PRAISE FOR THIS BOOK

Kept by God is a very important book. It is addressing one of the most asked questions in the Christian life and one that troubles many Christians at different points of their walk with the Lord. Jeff Robinson takes the issue head on and does so in a very biblical, accessible, and winsome way. The open dialogue format of this book makes it easy for anyone to engage, but also models for a pastor how to have a thoughtful conversation with a member of his flock who is asking the hard questions. I commend this book as well as the full series.

—Brian Croft

Executive Director, Practical Shepherding

Dr. Jeff Robinson is spot-on in recognizing that assurance of salvation is one of the main issues believers bring to their pastor. It is certainly consistent with my experience in thirty-eight years of pastoral ministry. Though the lack of assurance may present in many ways, it is the same question at the core: 'Am I really saved?' Christians have often been taught to get their sense of assurance from their subjective experience of the gospel. Jeff focuses on the objective nature of the gospel to help believers see that their faith rests on something outside themselves that never changes, not inside themselves and ever changing. Strangely, yet delightfully, assurance comes from not thinking about what we have done but focusing on what Jesus has done.

—Dr. Tony Rose

Retired pastor, Founder T. R. Relational Leadership

The biblical teaching on the certainty of completing the journey heavenward by true believers is beautiful, encouraging, God-glorifying, and an indispensable element of the clear biblical manifestation of the gracious power by which God saves sinners-- "By grace are ye saved." It is not a mere optional appendage to evangelical soteriological assertions but embodies the whole of revelation concerning sin, God's covenantal fidelity, the work of the Spirit, the person of Christ, the intention of the cross, resurrection, ascension, and session of Christ. Jeff Robinson has unfolded beautifully the wonder and essentiality of this doctrine powerfully in this book. Writing in a dialogic fashion, the author has tackled every nuance of objection to the doctrine and explored the coherent, integrated beauty of its place in Reformed biblical theology. He has used every strength of his rich preparation for writing this book. He shows the clarity of a journalist, the tenderness of a pastor, the awareness of a historian, the integrative capacity of a theologian, the prowess of a biblical interpreter, and the humility of a creature who is fully aware of his fallen state. Buy and read this book as an investment in the grace of growing in the knowledge of our Lord and Savior, Jesus Christ.

—Tom Nettles
Church Historian and Author

As a pastor, I know first-hand the death-grip that fear has on many Christians. They look at the world and feel paralyzing fear and they look at their lives and feel more of the same. There seems to be a pervasive sense that God doesn't really love them. *Kept By God* reminds readers that Christians can have confidence that God does indeed love them because of the work of Jesus Christ. Not only does He love them now, but He's promised to always love His people and will surely keep them to the end. Written with a pastor's heart and a conversational style, this book is a welcomed addition to those I'll have on hand at our church and in my counseling office.

—Matt Rogers

Pastor of Christ Fellowship Cherrydale amd Author

Kept by God: Perseverance by His Power is a deeply engaging and pastorally rich exploration of one of the most comforting doctrines in the Christian faith, the perseverance of the saints. Written as a dialogue between a pastor and a young believer, the book brings profound theological truths to life in a conversational, accessible way. Jeff Robinson combines biblical clarity, historical insight, and pastoral warmth to help readers see that salvation is not merely begun by God but sustained by His sovereign grace. This book will encourage weary Christians, equip pastors, and strengthen the church to rest confidently in the God who saves and keeps His people forever.

—Dave Kiehn

Pastor of Park Baptist Church

KEPT BY GOD

KEPT
BY GOD

Perseverance by His Power

Jeff Robinson

Dedication

Dedicated to the memory of the late Harry L. Reeder and R. C. Sproul, two titans of evangelical ministry whose lives and preaching/teaching ministry shaped my own, two men whose works continue to make sublime truths clear such that all Christians, regardless of their education level, can learn about and rejoice in the towering truths of sacred Scripture. Only eternity will tell how much you both helped this Baptist minister and thousands more like me.

Kept by God: Perseverance by His Power

© 2025 Jeff Robinson

ISBN 978-1-955295-78-9

Cover Design: Rachel Rosales
Typesetting: Rachel Rosales
Editing: Lauren Spano

COURIER PUBLISHING

100 Manly Street
Greenville, South Carolina 29601

Printed in the United States of America

Table of Contents

Foreword

Pastoral questions run the gamut. From moral quandaries to life decisions to theological struggles, inquiring members regularly test their pastors' theological mettle. Most pressing for clear answers will be matters of the soul. It's one thing to offer advice on a job prospect or a college to attend or the difference between Baptists and Jehovah's Witnesses, but quite another when one's relationship to Christ comes to the forefront. Here pastors must be sharpened by years of study, prayer, and practice over God's Word to give a word in season for members of the flock. They must speak patiently, carefully, and winsomely if they will serve their flock. That's especially the case when addressing young Christians whose spiritual acumen and discernment is still developing.

With these cases, I've found dialogical models of pastoral counsel to be most useful in shaping my understanding of how to address theological matters that run to the core of a congregation's life. Reading, for instance, John Newton's conversations with John Ryland Jr. has captivated and reordered the way I approach pastoral conversations. Their discussions and others sharpen my pastoral ability to speak with clarity and compassion with those I'm shepherding.

That's why this series from Courier Publishing, *Dialogues in Doctrine*, catches my eye. With trusted authors who write from depths of theological reflection and tested experience in pastoral counsel, each volume picks up common questions faced in every pastor's ministry. With the initial book addressing assurance and the question of a Christian losing his salvation, others will follow that carry the same heightened need for the Christian's understanding: God's providence, election and predestination, the end times, and more.

Dialogues in Doctrine's approach doesn't leave readers on a limb trying to sort through dense theological arguments. Series editor Jeff Robinson calls the approach "a dialogical theology." By that, the deep dive into theological answers comes via conversational style. Through the framework of an ongoing discussion with a young Christian, the authors listen to the doctrinal questions from the young Christian, probe for more insight in the young Christian's query, and then respond with the kind of dialogue that a thoughtful pastor might initiate. Working through the breadth of the doctrine in question, the authors delve into biblical explanation, systematic theology, historical theology, biblical theology, and pastoral application.

Aside from its welcomed readability, what makes *Dialogues in Doctrine* so useful is its appropriateness for both pastors and church members. It shows the importance of life-on-life when helping those struggling through soul and doctrinal issues, while cutting no corners in offering biblical and theological clarity. The series will offer books that I will happily give to those I'm shepherding to answer doctrinal questions, guide biblical/theological investigation, and to discuss for application. As a pastor, I will profit by the wisdom of those authoring the series, as they help to tightly argue biblical truths in a winsome, personable manner.

Series editor Jeff Robinson's initial volume, *Kept by God: Perseverance by His Power*, tackles the sticky question of assurance of salvation. Can a Christian lose his/her salvation? With pastoral warmth, Jeff works through Scripture to give his imaginary inquirer solid biblical tracks to continue to run on beyond the discussion with the pastor. Jeff's theological precision shows through in the documents and books from which he draws pithy statements and explanations to round out his biblical discussion. Wisely demonstrating how a pastor might question and probe without come across as an FBI agent, he gives readers a chance to sift through their understanding of biblical explanations. Like the approach of historical models in theological dialogue by John Gerstner, C. S. Lewis, Andrew Fuller, and John Newton, he gives pastors a workable model for how to do the same in their setting.

I met Jeff in the 90s and we immediately found a common bond in love for the gospel, the church, church history, and the church's mission. His expertise in historical theology has been a well that I've often drawn from to help me work through questions in my church context. That's another reason I'm thrilled by the initial volume and the ones to come in this *Dialogues in Doctrine* series. Seasoned pastors who know how to explain the doctrines of the faith, not simply to improve academic understanding but to apply doctrine to the whole of life, make this series a gold mine for strengthening the health of local churches. Jeff's vision for *Dialogues in Doctrine* will be greatly appreciated by pastors and church members—young and old. Plus, the books in the series will be wonderful tools for members to share their faith and encourage fellow believers by inviting others to read through the books and discuss their content.

After you read the first installment in the series, like me, I'm confident you'll want to pick up those that follow. You will find them to be trusted sources in biblical dialogue for church members to be built up in the Christian faith.

—Phil A. Newton, Ph.D.
Retired Lead Pastor; Director of Pastoral Care & Mentoring for The Pillar Network, Visiting Professor of Pastoral Theology at Southeastern Baptist Theological Seminary, Author of Courier Publishing titles Mending the Nets; Are You a Christian?; *and* Unburdening the Soul

Dialogues in Doctrine
Volume 1

Introduction

If there were a hall-of-fame for popular questions that Christians ask their pastor, surely the first inductee would be some version of this important query: Can a Christian lose their salvation? In other words, can a person, once regenerated by God's grace and indwelt by the Holy Spirit, backslide away from Christ to such a degree that they forfeit eternal life and are lost in the end?

The short and overwhelmingly biblical answer to the question is no. However, in the history of the church, Christians have not agreed on that answer. Numerous evangelical denominations, most of whom we might label "Arminian" (and we will in this work in contrast to Reformed views) due to historical connections to the figure who stands at the fountainhead of final apostasy for the believer, argue that it is possible for a gen-uine Christian to fall into such a grievous state of patterned sinfulness (or commit what might be called a "big ticket" sin against the Ten Com-mandments such as adultery or murder) that they will "lose out" with God in the end.

However, James Petigru Boyce, founding president of The Southern Baptist Theological Seminary, states clearly the doctrine that will be argued in this book:

> ...not one will finally apostatize or be lost; but each will assuredly persevere and be saved. This fact is taught explicitly in the word of God, which sets it forth as due to the purpose and power of God and the grace which he bestows, and now to any excellence or power in the be-liever. Indeed, such as is stated to be the weakness of man that, if left to himself, he would assuredly fall, against the dan-ger of which he is constantly warned; a danger to which even the best instructed and most sanctified are liable. . . (Boyce, *Abstract*, 426)

This book is the first in a series and will follow a methodology that differs profoundly from most books that systematically examine biblical doctrines, but one that has a long and happy legacy in the history of the church. This work—and the series that will arise afterward—is what might best be called a dialogical theology. The exposition of this doctrine and the handling of objections to it will unfold as a lengthy conversation between a pastor and a parishioner—as if a church member is struggling with the question at hand. It will systematically deal with all the issues and common questions related to the doctrine of perseverance of the saints and will dabble in a related conversation on a believer's assurance.

This book and the upcoming series were inspired by the work of John Gerstner, a theologian who mentored one of my ministry heroes, R. C. Sproul. Gerstner's book, *Theology and Dialogue*, is a systematic theology that unfolds as a conversation between a teacher and an inquirer. It is a brilliant approach to take the core doctrines of the historic Christian faith and make them clearly understandable and applicable to the lives of ordinary, non-seminary educated Christians.

Gerstner was by no means the first to harness dialogue in service of theology; C. S. Lewis used a form of dialogue creatively in numerous of his works, including my favorite of his writings, *The Screwtape Letters*. Similarly, the great Baptist theologian, Andrew Fuller, used dialogue in a doctrinal debate with General Baptist pastor Dan Taylor. The two debated in letters the issue of whether or not every single person has a duty to repent from his sin and believe in Christ, even those who are not regenerated by the Holy Spirit and thus have no ability to repent and believe. Their letters back and forth, published in Fuller's Works as *Reply to Philanthropos*, provide us with clarity on an issue that is widely debated among evangelical Christians.

About *Dialogues in Doctrine*

A few years ago, R. C. Sproul wrote a popular introduction to theology titled, *Everyone's a Theologian: An Introduction to Systematic Theology* (Reformation Trust, 2014). The book is aimed at readers who are at least relatively new to studying theology, particularly systematic theology which, with all its categories and terms—prolegomena, anthropology, soteriology, pneumatology, and the like—can be intimidating for the first-time theologizer. Most Christians don't wake up every morning thinking deeply about the hypostatic union.

But Sproul rightly argues, as the title suggests, that every single person is a theologian—
Christian or not. As soon as you say "I don't believe in God" or "I just believe in Jesus, but am
not interested in theology," you've made a couple
of deeply theological statements. Theology is often seen as the domain of the Bible scholar or the
seminary student, but not the average Christian.
Like Sproul's book (and really, his entire ministry
at Ligonier), the target reader of this book and
the ensuing series is the person who has not had
opportunity to study theology formally. The target audience is what a good friend of mine calls
"folks," that is, ordinary Christians who want to
dive into the Bible more deeply but might be
afraid of studying theology.

I agree with Dr. Sproul that everyone is a
theologian. We all have thoughts and opinions
about God and sin and death and what's wrong
with this world and where we've come from and
where humanity is ultimately going. There are answers to all those questions that are biblical and
beautiful; there are answers that are misguided
and downright frightening. If you are a theologian—and you are—I want you to be a good
theologian. What makes one a good theologian?
Seeking to be rigorously biblical, and unstintingly

faithful to God's inspired, inerrant, authoritative, all-sufficient Word.

So, the aim of this book and the ensuing series is to provide both pastors and laypersons with an accessible volume that teases out each doctrine under consideration and handles common objections. A back-and-forth dialogue makes it easy to handle questions as they might naturally arise between a pastor and a parishioner or a Christian and a skeptic on the issues at hand, making the volumes helpful, I hope, for both pastors, church members, and the newcomer to the study of theology. I want these books to help pastors explain and apply doctrines and also serve as a resource a pastor might give to someone wrangling with these teachings after he's had a conversation with that church member or prospective church member.

While these works are not academic in nature, the conversations will include quotations and insights from sound biblical scholars and from key figures in church history, so it will include footnoted sources for further study and investigation of the topics. All this will be enfolded into the conversations between a young Christian and their pastor. I hope you find this approach easily accessible, clear, compelling, and helpful.

Like many readers, I am a verbal processor and tend to hammer out big issues in conversations with others, which is why I think this approach has potential to help everyday Christians and ministers called to shepherd them.

CHAPTER 1

Lest We Drift Away from It: Can I Lose My Salvation?

When I fear my faith will fail,
Christ will hold me fast;
When the tempter would prevail,
He will hold me fast.

I could never keep my hold,
through life's fearful path;
For my love is often cold;
He must hold me fast.[1]

"Perseverance of the saints is a truth which the natural heart has bitterly opposed in every age."[2]

---

[1] Keith and Kristyn Getty, "He Will Hold Me Fast"

[2] J. C. Ryle, Old Paths (Louisville, KY: GLH Publishing, 2021), 214.

Young Christian

Good morning, pastor. Do you have some time? I am wrestling with an issue that has kept me up at night, an issue I have discussed with other believers and a couple of others in ministry, but I have gotten very different answers from each. I've also been reading the Bible, and while it seems to present a clear answer, sometimes it doesn't seem to square with what I've seen in other people who claim to be Christians. And there are some passages that seem unclear to me.

Pastor

Of course, I'm happy to help with your question, what is it?

Young Christian

Can a Christian lose their salvation? By this, I mean a person who seems to have really given their life to the Lord and have walked with him for a while, maybe even many years. Eventually, they either walk away from the faith or they fall into some grievous sin and never return to the Lord. And I've met some who, though they seem to have been converted, never gain assurance of their faith. Yet, I read in the Bible things like no one ever being able to snatch them out of God's hands, so I'm confused.

Pastor

Well, I think the Bible gives some clear answers to this. In a word, no, I do not believe a person who has been genuinely converted to Christ by the grace of God, has been a recipient of the new birth, will ever finally fall away from the faith. I love how our confession of faith, written way back in 1689, puts it. Let me read it to you:

> Those whom God has accepted in the beloved, effectually called and sanctified by his Spirit, and given the precious faith of his elect unto, can neither totally nor finally fall from the state of grace, but shall certainly persevere therein to the end, and be eternally saved, seeing the gifts and callings of God are without repentance, from which source he still begets and nourishes in them faith, repentance, love, joy, hope, and all the graces of the Spirit unto immortality; and though many storms and floods arise and beat against them, yet they shall never be able to take them off that foundation and rock

which by faith they are fastened upon; notwithstanding, through unbelief and the temptations of Satan, the sensible sight of the light and love of God may for a time be clouded and obscured from them, yet he is still the same, and they shall be sure to be kept by the power of God unto salvation, where they shall enjoy their purchased possession, they being engraved upon the palm of his hands, and their names having been written in the book of life from all eternity.

Young Christian

Wow, that's beautiful. There's so much packed into that paragraph. I'll admit, sometimes I doubt my salvation and wonder if I'm going to lose it when I sin. I was talking to another believer the other day at work, and she was telling me that she believes she was saved at age six, lost her salvation during the teenage years because she spent a few years living in rebellion before getting saved again after college. She said that a true Christian will not sin.

Pastor

What do you make of all that? Did you find it compelling?

Young Christian

Well, my life has been like my coworker's to a degree. I walked the aisle during a revival meeting when I was 10 and it seemed like I was a believer until I got to about 17. I started sinning in ways it seems a true Christian would not, and that lasted into college. Even now, there are times when I'm kind of lukewarm toward the things of God. And I still sin and get very frustrated that I do. Too often, it seems like I don't do what I want to do, and I have to ask God to forgive me. But is that the behavior of a genuine believer? I have a hard time believing that a Christian would want to sin like that.

Pastor

Well, you raise many important questions, all great questions for sure. Your questions are very common. In the many years I've been a pastor, I've been asked these questions probably more than any others. It's common for Christians to wonder if they've lost their salvation or even if they were ever converted to Christ at all. If we're honest, every Christian has probably wrestled with them at some time in their walk with the Lord.

We're all dogged by sin. Actually, the Bible says Christians face three enemies, sometimes called the unholy trinity: the world, the flesh, and the devil. Romans 12:1-2 says the world wants to press us into its God-denying mold. Romans 7 tells us that an internal war between indwelling sin and the indwelling Spirit will rage within us until we reach our final home in glory. Even Jesus was confronted by Satan, whom the entire New Testament depicts as the enemy of our souls. In John 10:10, Jesus calls Satan a thief who works day and night to steal, kill, and destroy our faith. With those dark agents working against us, if we could lose our salvation, it is virtually certain that we would.

Young Christian

Have you ever doubted your salvation? You're a pastor, so I'm sure you have security that maybe regular believers lack.

Pastor

I have doubted it, for sure. Pastors are just like "ordinary" Christians except that they are called to vocational ministry. Pastors are men in the middle of their sanctification just like the members whom they are called to shepherd. I have doubted, but after studying Scripture, I've never been under the impression that I've lost my salvation. Those three enemies about which I just spoke have caused me to question at time whether I was ever converted in the first place.

Young Christian

It seems that Christians disagree on the answer to this question. I know it matters practically, because it seems like I'll never gain assurance that I'm a genuine believer if I don't believe I am secure in my salvation. But doctrinally, does it really matter? Isn't this one of those things that is, as I heard someone at church say once, a matter indifferent, a thing on which good men can just agree to disagree?

Pastor

Actually, it is very important. If a true believer can be lost at the last, then it really changes the character of God. It really undermines what Jesus did at the cross and it undermines the ongoing work he is doing for us right now as we have this discussion—he is at the Father's right hand praying for us. It also undermines many, many promises in Scripture that have provided a security blanket of comfort for believers for centuries. It is an important doctrine. I'm not ready to say that someone who believes in the possibility of final apostasy is engaging in heresy, but I would say it is decidedly dangerous to deny the believer's perseverance. It's far more serious than, say, disagreeing on matters such as the timing of the Lord's return or which Bible translation one should use.

Young Christian
Why do you suppose some Christians believe salvation can be lost?

Pastor
It's hard to tell, but experience tells me that it comes from a misunderstanding of how we "stay" saved and also the full biblical and theological witness to the perseverance of the saints. There's a lot more to this than I can answer right now, but if you're willing, we could meet together and make this the subject of more intensive, in-depth biblical and theological study. Would you like that?

Young Christian
Oh, absolutely. Anything that's going to help my walk with the Lord and teach me more about the central doctrines of the Christian faith.

Pastor
Well, let's plan on having several talks about this. We'll talk about the Bible, theology, even church

history. I'll walk you through the major things the Bible makes clear about our perseverance, how it relates to the other core doctrines of our faith, and what other solid teachers from the past have said more clearly and powerfully than I ever could.

Here's what I think you will find as we undertake this study: Perseverance of the saints might better be termed "preservation of the saints." I say that because God saves us and keeps us saved. He uses numerous means to accomplish our perseverance, but it's still his work. We are kept by God. I think there's disagreement within the body of Christ because there's a failure to see that perseverance is also the gift of God—just like salvation. God saves us and keeps us saved. Over the years, the majority of churches within evangelicalism have focused more on man's response to God in salvation and perseverance than in God's unilateral grace in saving us and his work to keep us in his grace. These two different theologies the great reformer Martin Luther, one of several great men we'll meet from church history, called a theology of glory versus a theology of the cross. In a theology of glory—or theology from below—man is the deciding factor in our response to God's offer of grace. In a theology of the cross—or a theology from above—God saves and grants perseverance through the means he's ordained to accomplish final salvation. Does that make sense?

Here's the way an old theologian whom I read puts it: "It is, strictly speaking, not man but God who perseveres. Perseverance may be defined as that continuous operation of the Holy Spirit in the believer, by which the work of grace that is begun in the heart, is continued and brought to completion. It is because God never forsakes His work that believers continue to stand to the very end."[3] I'd summarize the Bible's teaching this way, and this should be of great comfort for us: God saves us and keeps us saved. The promise in Philippians 1:6 undergirds this great truth: "And I am sure of this, that he who began a good work in you will bring it to completion at the day of Christ Jesus."

Young Christian

I really look forward to diving into this. I can see how those are different views. It seems like Luther was saying either man is in control or God is in control.

---

[3] Louis Berkhof, *Systematic Theology* (Carlisle, PA: Banner of Truth, 1998), 546.

Pastor

Exactly. You're off to a good start. Let's start by looking at what Scripture says about perseverance and apostasy. We always start with Scripture because it is the inspired, inerrant, authoritative Word of the living God. Sacred Scripture is a Christian's final authority. Scripture speaks God's words and we submit ourselves to it. Plain and simple.

Questions for
Further Reflection

1. Do you know a person who once claimed to be a follower of Jesus Christ who seems to have fallen away? Discuss those circumstances to determine why the issue of perseverance is so troubling to some Christians.

2. Why does the pastor say we are "kept by God?" How is that different than saying that a Christian keeps himself in the Lord?

3. How does the pastor define perseverance? Do you find his definition compelling?

CHAPTER 2

We Are Kept by God

Fear not, I am with you.
Oh, be not dismayed, for I am your God
and will still give you aid;
I'll strengthen you, help you, and cause you to stand,
Upheld by my righteous, omnipotent hand.
That soul, though all hell, should endeavor to shake;
I'll never, no, never, no, never forsake.[1]

Pastor

To begin, let's make a positive biblical case, and then we can deal with some problem passages that seem to warn Christians of the possibility

---

[1] "How Firm a Foundation," author unknown, taken from John Rippon's *Selection of Hymns*

of falling away. I think the first thing a Christian must realize is that God both saves him and keeps him saved. God is sovereign in both his salvation and in his perseverance. The best place to start in theology is with God. Too often, we want to start with us, yet Scripture starts and concludes with God. The Bible makes it clear that God causes true believers to perservere even through many dangers, toils, and snares, which we'll get to later.

Young Christian
So, we don't start with man even though man is the one who is seeking to remain saved?

Pastor
Good theology always starts with God. Bad theology starts with man. The great reformer Martin Luther distinguished between a theology of glory and a theology of the cross, a distinction between theologies that begin and end with man and theologies that begin and end with God. Arminianism is a good example of a theology that centers on man. Instead of focusing on the sovereignty of God, Arminianism tends to focus on man's responsibility. But a God-centered theology, such as the great doctrines recovered in the Protestant Reformation, argues that salvation begins with

God, continues with God, and ends with God. As Jonah put it in Jonah 2:9, just before the big fish spat him out on dry land at the command of God, "salvation belongs to the LORD." True Christians are saved and stay saved thanks to the power of God. For the sake of simplicity, I'll refer to the view that accepts the possibility that a genuine Christian can forfeit his salvation as the Arminian position. I'll explain why that's historically accurate a bit later and hopefully that will assure you that I'm not merely broad-brushing a whole segment of evangelical Christianity.

Young Christian
I've been studying the Gospel of John lately. That might be a good place to start since Jesus speaks so much about salvation.

Pastor
Indeed, it is. John 3:16 is famous in promising eternal life to all who believe in Christ. It seems to me that it's illogical to see eternal life as just that if it is possible for a person to forfeit it. That would be eternal life maybe—unless I decide to walk away from it, don't you think?

Young Christian

Yes, it makes sense. Wouldn't it turn the phrase "eternal life" into nonsense if it weren't eternal life? That would seem like God is just playing games with us. He saves us, but we must keep ourselves saved.

Pastor

That's good thinking. Jesus promises eternal life to all who believe. That would seem to be a flimsy promise that's really "eternal life possibly." John 10 is a piece of strong evidence to my main contention in this conversation that God saves us and then causes us to persevere in his grace. It's true that genuine saints persevere all the way to the end, and it's equally true that we are kept by God.

In John 10, Jesus gives an extended exposition of himself as the good shepherd. In John 10:9, Jesus speaks of himself as the door of the sheep pen and concludes, "If anyone enters by me, he will be saved and will come in and out and find pasture." You see how straight-forward that is?

Young Christian

What do you mean?

Pastor

Jesus says those who are saved will find pasture. There's no conditional clause there. Then in John 10:11, he says, "I am the good shepherd. The good shepherd lays down his life for the sheep." So, Jesus dies for those who are his. Follow the logic here? He doesn't lay down his life for everybody, but for the sheep—his people. In verse 14, he says, "I know my own and they know me." He knows his people and they know him—his redeemed people. To point out something important here: this seems to demand definite atonement—the truth that Jesus actually accomplished the salvation of his elect at Calvary. But that's another discussion for another day.

The central truth I'm driving at in our current conversation is found in John 10:27-29:

> My sheep hear my voice, and I know them, and they follow me. I give them eternal life, and they will never perish, and no one will snatch them out of my hand. My Father, who has given them to me, is greater than all, and no one is able to snatch them out the Father's hand.

You see what he's saying here? It seems to be clear: The Lord gives his sheep the endless life of fellowship with God. He protects them from perishing, according to the invincible nature of divine grace. And he allows no one to snatch them out of his almighty hand. Jesus here summarizes what I'm trying to show you as being the clear teaching of sacred Scripture: the saints persevere because God preserves them. They are not even able to snatch themselves out of God's hand—why would a true Christian even want to? Answer? They won't. Jesus is the great Shepherd of the sheep. He will save them and keep them saved, protecting them from all wolves who will try to snatch them away. The Shepherd's hand is also Father's hand, and the supreme power of God is the ultimate guarantee of the sheep's safety.

This is exactly what Jesus had in mind earlier in John 6:38-39 where he's teaching his disciples what he meant in calling himself "the bread of life." There, he told them (and us) this:

> For I have come down from heaven, not to do my own will but the will of him who sent me. And this is the will of him who sent me, that I should lose nothing

of all that he has given me but raise it up
on the last day.

Jesus will lose none of his people. He will,
beyond the shadow of any doubt, raise them up
on the last day—this speaks to our resurrection
which was secured by his resurrection. God gra-
ciously ensures the final salvation of all his people. What do you think now?

Young Christian
I think God keeps his people saved! So, both the
Father and the Son are active in keeping the sheep
saved?

Pastor
Absolutely. The Spirit is involved, too. It is the
Spirit who works in sinful hearts to create repentance and faith. The Spirit indwells us and is active in keeping us on the King's Highway every
day of our lives. The entire godhead is unified
in saving us. What power on earth or in all of
creation is able to overcome that and snatch true
believers away? None. Paul actually takes this up
gloriously in Romans 8. Let's look at that next
since it seems to be a logical wrung to take next
up the ladder of this discussion.

Young Christian

Haven't parts of Romans been called the *Magna Carta* of our salvation?

Pastor

Indeed. *Magna Carta* is Latin for the Great Charter of Freedoms. The final paragraph in Romans 3 has been given that label, which is a fitting title because it expresses the gospel in explosive terms about Christ killing our sin and setting us free from sin, its penalty, its power. And Christ sets us free from the tyranny of death. It's beautiful, like every word of Paul's great letter to the Romans. Chapter 8 may be the Mount Olympus of theology written by Paul's inspired pen.

The discussion really begins in Romans 8:28-30 where Paul says God causes all things to work together for the Christian's good—to all who are "called according to his purpose." This last phrase refers to God's effectual call which goes out through gospel proclamation. God's chosen children respond to the call—by God's grace they hear and come to Christ, drawn effectually by the Holy Spirit's power. Then in verses 29-30 Paul links up what the Puritans often called the Golden Chain of Salvation with every link serving as a critical part of Paul's overall argument for the believer's eternal security.

> For those whom he foreknew he also predestined to be conformed to the image of his Son, in order that he might be the firstborn among many brothers. And those whom he predestined he also called, and those whom he called he also justified, and those whom he justified he also glorified.

There it is: God effectually calls his people, those whom he predestined to salvation, he "foreknew" literally meaning he "knew" them—God had a relationship with them in eternity past. This "knowing" is the same relational "knowing" Adam had with Eve when they produced a son through procreation. It's not sexual but speaks of a deeply intimate relationship. So, he predestined them to be conformed to the image of Jesus—no losing out there. It was done before the world began. He called them, justified them—by faith—and will glorify them in eternity future. In one bold phrase Paul sets forth salvation past, salvation present, and salvation future, all accomplished by Christ and applied by Christ.

After that, in one of the most powerful paragraphs ever set to paper by a pen, Paul makes sure they know this salvation can never be taken away. His argument, for our purposes, begins in verse 33, "Who shall bring any charge against God's elect? It is God who justifies." Once a believer is justified by faith in Christ, he or she is declared righteous (an argument we will get to later) and is declared not guilty in the heavenly courtroom since Christ bore his or her guilt. Paul is here saying, there are no longer any charges that can be successfully lodged against saved sinners. Once God justifies a sinner, they are justified forever.

He elevates the argument in verse 34a: "Who is to condemn?" As he said earlier in Romans, there is no condemnation for those who are in Christ Jesus. None. Not now, not ever. Why? Because Jesus is at the Father's right hand praying for his people, interceding for them. And, as we will discuss in greater length later, Christ always gets what he prays for, or else he would be fallible, and we know that a fallible Christ is no Christ at all.

Then, Paul's words grow even more powerful and poetic. Verse 35 until the end of chapter 8 represents one of the most beautiful paragraphs ever written and they speak to the believer's security—in very clear and unforgettable terms. Paul's

logic is edifying and easy to follow. He starts with
the question in verse 35: "Who shall separate us
from the love of Christ? Shall tribulation, or dis-
tress, or persecution, or famine, or nakedness, or
danger, or sword?" In other words, can all the bad
things, all the adversity a believer can face in life
remove him from God's love? Then Paul further
answers the question by quoting the Old Testament, Psalm 44:22 in this case: "For your sake
we are being killed all day long; we are regard-
ed as sheep to be slaughtered." In other words,
suffering is the common lot of Christians in this
fallen world just as it was for Israel in the Old
Testament. Will those things separate us from the
love of Christ?

He answers over the final three verses (37-
39)—and what glorious words:

> No, in all these things we are more than
> conquerors through him who loved us.
> For I am sure that neither death nor life,
> nor rulers, nor things present nor things
> to come, nor powers, not height nor
> depth, nor anything else in all creation,
> will be able to separate us from the love
> of God in Christ Jesus our Lord.

Did you catch that? He said nothing in all creation, nothing at all, can separate a genuine believer from the love of God. Come what may, by God's grace, we are more than conquerors through Christ. If we could lose our salvation, we would, but Christ is strong, and he makes us more than conquerors.

What do you think of that beautifully-worded promise? We are kept by grace.

Young Christian
Wow, that is very clear. Beautiful. But what about perseverance from the human end? Can I walk away from the love of God? I have some relatives who have made that argument. They say, "Yes, but you can remove yourself from God's hand. John and Paul are talking about salvation from God's perspective. From a human perspective, we can walk away."

Pastor
Are you part of God's creation?

Young Christian
I am.

Pastor

Paul here says nothing in all creation can cause God to remove his love from his people. So, no, you are unable to successfully remove yourself from God's redeeming love. It is God, in his love for us who keeps us. I think part of the problem is the terminology we use to describe the saint's security.

Young Christian

What do you mean by that? Do you mean eternal security? Do you think calling it that is a problem?

Pastor

I do. I think the term itself has been misused by some popular evangelical pastors and authors to give the impression that a Christian can make a profession of faith and then go live any way they desire and still expect to be with the Lord on the last day. Salvation, by some accounts, does not necessarily lead to sanctification. Now let me be clear. We are not saved by sanctification, but, and this is important, a genuine believer will live on some level like a follower of Jesus Christ. We'll get to that later. But I think a better, more accurate, more historically-venerated term for this is perseverance of the saints, which, I would argue also includes God's preservation of the saints.

Young Christian

What is the difference between perseverance and eternal security?

Pastor

It is certainly true that a genuine believer is eternally secure, but I think it's better to say a genuine believer will persevere in the faith, even through temptations and backslidings, until the end. Salvation is monergistic—God does it all. Sanctification is synergistic: we cooperate with God in our daily transformation after having received the new birth. Our confession of faith—the Second London Confession gives an excellent, full, clear definition:

> Those whom God hath accepted in the beloved, effectually called and sanctified by his Spirit, and given the precious faith of his elect unto, can neither totally nor finally fall from the state of grace, but shall certainly persevere therein to the end, and be eternally saved, seeing the gifts and callings of God are without repentance,

whence he still begets and nourisheth in them faith, repentance, love, joy, hope, and all the graces of the Spirit unto immortality; and though many storms and floods arise and beat against them, yet they shall never be able to take them off that foundation and rock which by faith they are fastened upon; notwithstanding, through unbelief and the temptations of Satan, the sensible sight of the light and love of God may for a time be clouded and obscured from them, yet he is still the same, and they shall be sure to be kept by the power of God unto salvation, where they shall enjoy their purchased possession, they being engraven upon the palm of his hands, and their names having been written in the book of life from all eternity. (Chapter 17, Paragraph 1)

Paragraph three of the confession addresses the reality that sin, temptation, and suffering will harass Christians as they live in this fallen world, yet God will cause them to stand eternally in the face of it all:

And though they may, through the temptation of Satan and of the world, the prevalency of corruption remaining in them, and the neglect of means of their preservation, fall into grievous sins, and for a time continue therein, whereby they incur God's displeasure and grieve his Holy Spirit, come to have their graces and comforts impaired, have their hearts hardened, and their consciences wounded, hurt and scandalize others, and bring temporal judgments upon themselves, yet shall they renew their repentance and be preserved through faith in Christ Jesus to the end.

The authors of our confession follow Scripture in anticipating that weak, fallen people, even redeemed people, will wrangle with sin over the course of a lifetime of walking with Christ. Their sins will come with consequences, but the indwelling Spirit of God will renew them to repentance again and again. That's really the difference between Christians and non-Christians: Christians have new hearts and desire holy things, non-Christians do not. When Christians fall into sin, even a prolonged backslidden condition, they do not like it. Unbelievers sin boldly and have no remorse whatsoever when it comes to whether or not they've offended God.

Young Christian
So, you're saying that we are kept by God. I see that. Are there other places in Scripture that teach divine preservation?

Pastor
Too many for me to unpack in what is supposed to be a series of brief conversations, but here's another from the apostle Paul, this one found in the benediction in 1 Thessalonians 5:23-24:

> Now may the God of peace himself sanctify you completely and may your whole spirit and soul and body be kept blameless at the coming of our Lord Jesus Christ. He who calls you is faithful; he will surely do it.

Don't miss this: God will keep His people completely until the second coming of Christ. That's a promise: "he will surely do it." If true believers can fall from grace, Paul could not—and would not—say that. A. W. Pink summarizes this comforting promise well:

> The Apostle's confidence in the absolute security of believers was founded not on the strength of their resolutions or ability to persevere, but on the veracity of Him that cannot lie. Since God has promised to His Son a certain people for His inheritance, to deliver them from sin and condemnation, and to make them participants of eternal life in glory, it is certain that He will not allow any of them to perish.[2]

I Peter 1:3-5 also contains a beautiful promise of God's preserving grace for his redeemed people:

> He has caused us to be born again . . . to an inheritance that is imperishable, undefiled, and unfading, kept in heaven for you, who by God's power are being guarded through faith for a salvation to be revealed in the last time.

---

[2] A. W. Pink, *The Attributes of God* ebook (New Dehli: Digital Fire, 2024), loc. 1011.

If God is guarding our inheritance in heaven, then asserting that free will can lead one to lose his salvation seems to strengthen the power of man and weaken the power of God, not to mention what it means for Peter's language to describe the inheritance as "imperishable, undefiled, and unfading."

Wouldn't you say those words ring with an empty note if it is possible for human beings to undermine them? Are we stronger than God? No way. The word translated "guarded" there is a military term used to connate a military position an army defends and holds no matter the cost. We have an inheritance in heaven – one we cannot throw away like empty Taco Bell wrappers. That inheritance is not here on earth, but is in heaven and God is guarding it, keeping it for us, at all cost. It will be revealed in the last day. If Arminians are correct, then we might as well cut that passage out of the Bible and throw it away because Peter is lying to us.

Perseverance isn't only a New Testament doctrine. It is found throughout the Old Testament, too. Look at Psalm 37:28, for example: "For the LORD loves justice; he will not forsake his saints. They are preserved forever, but the children of the wicked shall be cut off." Doesn't get much clearer than that.

Here's a quote I recently read that beautifully summarizes God's preservation of his saints: "God will never give up on you. His grace is so high that you can't get over it, so deep that you can't possibly get under it, and so tenacious that you can't get away from it."[3]

Young Christian

You seem to be saying that if we can lose our salvation, then God isn't really telling us the truth when he promises us grace.

Pastor

That's exactly what I'm saying. God's children are not able to defeat his love for them. John 13:1b tells us, "Having loved his own which were in the world, he loved them to the end." The love God has for us is in Christ Jesus, in God's Son. We did nothing to attract the love of God to us in the first place—it was all of grace. There was nothing in us that would commend us to the Lord. Since we did nothing to attract God's electing love, we can do nothing to repel it. Think about your earthly

---

[3] Neil C. Stewart, "Our Future Hope," in Tabletalk Magazine, Ligonier Ministries, March 2025, p. 24.

parents. You are their son and they will love you no matter what. There is nothing you could do that would remove their love or cause you to no longer be their son. How much more our perfect Father?

Questions for
Further Reflection

1. How did Martin Luther distinguish between a theology of the cross and a theology of glory? How does that relate to the doctrine of perseverance?

2. How does John 3:16 teach perseverance?

3. How do we distinguish between good theology and bad theology?

4. What part of the Bible is often called the Magna Carta of our salvation? Why is it called that?

5. Why is 1 Peter 1:3-5 such a clear promise of perseverance for Christians? If a genuine believer could lose his salvation, how would we interpret this promise?

CHAPTER 3

They Went Away and Followed Him No More

Prone to wander, Lord I feel it,
Prone to leave the God I love;
Take my heart, Lord,
Take and seal it for thy courts above.[1]

Pastor

Today, I want us to look at a Bible text that really puts this issue into the proper biblical perspective. You might even say it is the key to understanding the full scriptural teaching on perseverance of the saints. Are you familiar with the parables of Jesus in the gospels?

---

[1] Robert Robinson, "Come, Thou Fount of Every Blessing"

Young Christian

Yes, they are among my favorite parts of the New Testament. I love how Jesus teaches doctrine through those stories. It helps me to understand what he's saying because the parables put the cookies on the shelf where all Christians can reach them.

Pastor

Before we do that, are there people whom you have encountered in church who seem to have been walking with the Lord at one time, but completely flipped and walk with him no more? Maybe witnessing their apostasy has made you wonder whether it's possible for a genuine Christian to lose out with the Lord in the end?

Young Christian

For sure. There was a man who was saved during a revival once and seemed to be on fire for the Lord as if he had been lit ablaze by the new birth. He shared the gospel with anyone who would listen and even started a layperson's evangelism ministry. He had many health issues and a group of well-meaning people in the church encouraged him to ask the Lord to heal him. He prayed and prayed about it, but when he continued to be sick, he totally abandoned what had been a fervent faith. He said since God wouldn't heal him, he wanted nothing to do with the Lord. I think some of those who encouraged him to pray for healing blamed him for not having enough faith to receive healing from the Lord.

Pastor
What did you think about that last part?

Young Christian
It sounded dangerous and unbiblical to me—to guarantee healing and then blame it on the man who failed to be healed.

Pastor
Indeed, it is. But the man who appeared to be a strong and solid convert never returned to the faith?

Young Christian
As far as I know, he didn't.

Pastor
Were there others?

Young Christian

Yes. There was a lady who served all the time in the women's ministry, who said she'd been saved as a little girl, and she fell into an adulterous affair and left with the new man and abandoned the faith at the same time. She claimed to have been a Christian for more than 30 years. These kinds of things really confuse me, a part of why I came to you in the first place.

Oh, and yes, there was a young man in the youth group whose Christian parents raised him in church. He was saved at age 11, but went off the college and his professors convinced him that the Christian faith is not true. Things like Darwinian evolution and the problem of evil led him to reject Christianity as intellectually untenable. He was a fine young man, and we all hated to see him go away like that. The elders have met with him, and the church regularly prays for him, but his heart is hardened to the Bible and the faith of his parents.

There was a man I once worked with for my company. He was a Christian and even led a Bible study at one time. He invested in stocks, was successful, and grew profoundly rich. His family bought a beach house and began to travel. He stopped going to church, stopped leading the

Bible study, and hasn't been part of a church in years. I saw him recently, and he said that in his success he had just outgrown any need for religion. I think money is now his functional god. It is tragic, but years ago, I would never have expected him to go away from the Lord.

Pastor

Remember, I asked if you were familiar with the parables of Jesus? Well, there's one in particular that I think helps us understand what happens when things happen as you've described, when people either fall into sin and leave the faith or just abruptly reject it to everyone's shock. The Parable of the Sower is well-known among Christians but isn't often considered in the discussion of final apostasy. It's important first to define what a parable is and what it is not. A parable is a story taken from real life (or a real-life situation) from which a moral or spiritual truth is drawn.[2] Parables are different from fables because a fable is not a real situation, it's more like fantasy, like Aesop's fables or *Lord of the Rings*. It's not exactly allegory either because in allegory like *Pilgrim's Progress*, every character or object in the story rep-

---

2 James Montgomery Boice, *The Parables of Jesus* (Chicago: Moody, 1983), 14.

resents something else. You can't press the details of a parable as far as you could in an allegory.

Basically, Jesus tells the Parable of the Sower about four different responses to the gospel. It's about a farmer who sows seed. This parable appears in Matthew, Mark, and Luke—the "Synoptic Gospels"—but I'm going to draw on Matthew's version.

Young Christian

So, this is going to relate to how we should assess those who apostatize from the faith?

Pastor

Yes. In this parable, Jesus begins by making clear that its topic is the word of the kingdom—the Word of God—and how it affects its hearers. The sower, or the farmer, goes out to plant seeds; some seeds fall along the path and the birds come and devour the seed. Some seeds fell on rocky ground where the soil was extremely shallow. The seed germinated and the plant came up quickly, but the sun rose and scorched the plant, killing it. Other seeds fell among thorns, and the thorns grew up and choked the life from the plant. Finally, there were seeds that fell in good soil and it produced much grain in varying amounts. Does it make sense so far?

Young Christian

Yes, it does.

Pastor

Jesus' disciples are baffled as to the meaning, so Jesus gives them the interpretation later in Matthew 13, after giving the purpose of parables. Jesus said he taught in parables to give light and understanding to some and to blind others to the truth, all of which is a sovereign, unilateral work of God.

The first seed, the one that fell along the path, Jesus said represents, "When anyone hears the word of the kingdom and does not understand it, the evil one comes and snatches away what has been sown in his heart" (Matt. 13:19). In other words, the gospel was preached and heard, but not believed. Satan blinds the eyes of the hearer, and he or she is not saved. This person is hard-hearted because of sin. This probably represents the vast majority of people who've ever lived since Genesis 3. But it's clear that this is not a person who was once saved and then abandoned the faith. Look at how Luke puts it: "The ones along the path are those who have heard; then the devil comes and takes away the word from their hearts, so that they may not believe and be saved" (Luke 8:12). You see that: "so that they may not believe" they may not have faith "and be saved." They never believed. They were in the realm of the gospel, but they never really gave their lives to it.

The second seed that fell from the farmer's sowing was planted on rocky ground. This person "hears the word and immediately receives it with joy, yet he has not root in himself, but endures for a while, and when tribulation or persecution arises on account of the word, immediately he falls away" (Matt. 13:20-21). Does that sound familiar, given the examples of apostasy you gave me earlier?

Young Christian
Yes, it really does. The first seed sounds like the young man who grew up in church but disbelieved once he went to college and heard arguments against the gospel from his professors. And the rocky ground sounds like the man who wasn't healed.

Pastor

The Bible anticipates the reality that some will walk with Jesus for only a little while. Now look at the third seed and soil: it is sown among thorns but is choked out by the deceitfulness of riches and the cares and turmoil of everyday life. The person with that heart is not saved because wealth, which is often a blessing from God, captivated his or her heart. Sometimes the cares of this world in the form of adversity or suffering can also cause a professing Christian to deny the faith. They wonder how a loving God could allow them to go through something so tragic and they reject the faith. But see, that person was never saved to begin with because what Jesus is here describing really is the condition of the hearts into which the seed of God's Word falls. Only one seed, the fourth one, fell into good soil—a heart that had been worked over in terms of repentance and faith by God's Holy Spirit and granted the new birth—and produced fruit, which we can assume is the fruit of the Holy Spirit which Paul outlines in Galatians 5.

Jesus gives us an unforgettable illustration of the unfruitful hearer in his encounter with the rich young man, a story found in three Gospels: Matthew, Mark, and Luke. The young man asks

Jesus the most vital question in human history: "What good deed must I do to have eternal life?" (Matt. 19:16). Jesus tells him he must keep the law perfectly or find salvation another way—and our Lord does this to show the young man that he has not in fact kept the law, despite the man's insistence that he has done so. Jesus exposes the idolatry of his heart: "Jesus said to him, 'If you would be perfect, go, sell what you possess and give to the poor, and you will have treasure in heaven; and come follow me'" (Matt. 19:21).

Jesus shows the folly of salvation by keeping the law and tells the young man to give his life to Christ. The young man's response offers a sobering picture of how the deceitfulness of riches can deafen one's spiritual hearing to the call of the gospel. That is precisely what Jesus speaks of with the third soil into which the gospel seed falls—that person shows a genuine interest in coming to Christ, but the cost is too high. It's like what Jesus said in Luke 14:25-33 about the cost of discipleship, which he summarizes in verse 33 by saying, "So therefore, any one of you who does not renounce all that he has cannot be my disciple." There can be a high cost to following Christ, and many aren't willing to pay it. As we sing in church, Jesus paid it all. Salvation is free and is gained by faith alone in Christ alone, but the journey with Christ may be rough in the same way the road Jesus walked—the Calvary road of suffering—came at a high cost.

Young Christian

The cost of discipleship almost never gets communicated when the gospel is preached. So, is that fourth soil, that fourth heart, where the seed bears much fruit, communicating that a genuine Christian will bear fruit and continue to bear fruit until the end of their journey on earth?

Pastor

Yes, but of course they can also be harassed by Satan and his minions, can even backslide for a time, or grow lukewarm for a time, but they will more or less bear fruit on some level until the end. If they slide back, they will return. The New Testament provides two major illustrations of this among Jesus' disciples: Judas Iscariot and Peter.

Judas was a disciple who, of course, betrayed Jesus. Some Arminian Christians argue that Judas was a genuinely converted follower of Christ who lost his faith and denied the Lord. However, this is clearly not the case as our Lord makes clear in his high priestly prayer in John 17; there, in verse 12, Jesus, speaking of his followers, says, "While I was with them, I kept them in your name, which you have given me. I have guarded them and not one of them has been lost except the son of destruction, *that the Scripture might be fulfilled.*" The "son of destruction" is Judas. His apostasy was prophesied in Psalm 41:9, "Even my close friend in whom I trusted, who ate my bread, has lifted up his heel against me." Judas fulfills the psalmist's prediction in John 13 when Jesus is with the twelve and tells them: "one of you will betray me." Judas, who kept the disciples' moneybag and often pilfered some of the funds for himself, ate the morsel which Jesus dipped; then Satan entered him and our Lord leaned over and whispered to him, "What you must do, do quickly." Judas left the disciples to go betray Jesus into the hands of the Sanhedrin.

Judas walked with Jesus for a while, but ultimately turned against him—exactly as was prophesied in the Old Testament. Judas wasn't an apostate. He was never a true believer. He even stole money from the disciples' moneybag, showing he was never on board with Christ.

Young Christian
What about Peter?

Pastor

Peter is the New Testament example of a backslidden follower of Jesus who repents and continues walking with the Lord. His story is well-known: Jesus tells the petulant Peter that he will deny the Lord three times leading up to his death at Calvary. Look how Jesus puts it in Luke 22:31-32: "Simon, Simon, behold, Satan demanded to have you, that he might sift you like wheat, but I have prayed for you that your faith may not fail. And when you have turned again, strengthen your brothers." Peter, of course, assured Jesus that his denial could ever happen: "Peter said to him, Lord, I am ready to go with you both to prison and to death." Jesus answers by getting right to the point of what Satan's sifting will entail: "Jesus said, I tell you, Peter, the rooster will not crow this day, until you deny me three times that you know me."

Of course, as Paul Harvey always loved to say, now we know the rest of the story; Peter denies Jesus three times, at the last cowering before a little girl who tries to finger him as one of Jesus' followers. But do you see the difference? What was the difference between Peter and Judas? What did Jesus do for Peter?

Young Christian

Jesus said he had prayed for Peter that his faith might not fail.

Pastor

That's exactly right. We will talk about this important doctrine and its tie to perseverance in greater depth later, but the theological reality is this: Jesus interceded for Peter and not for Judas. This is a clear instance of Jesus' intercessory work, his session before the Father in which he prays for all his people. And what happens to Peter because Jesus prayed for him?

Young Christian

Peter was restored, so he persevered. John's Gospel concludes with Jesus restoring Peter three times—one "Do you love me more than these, Peter?" for each of the three denials.

Pastor

You are learning quickly. That's exactly right. Because Jesus interceded for Peter, he did not finally and fully fall away as did Judas. Jesus is the infallible Son of God; he gets what he prays for, but more on that later. There were others who turned and walked away from Jesus.

Young Christian

Do you have in mind his followers in John 6?

Pastor

That's exactly what I have in mind. In John 6, Jesus issues one of his great "I Am" statements, saying "I am the bread of life." This comes on the heels of his having fed the 5,000, and he is interpreting that miracle's meaning for his followers. In John 6:60, Scripture says, "When many of his disciples heard of it, they said, 'This is a hard saying; who can listen to it?'" Jesus asks them, "Do you take offense at this?" (John 6:61c), before saying in verses 62-65, "It is the Spirit who gives life; the flesh is no help at all. The words that I have spoken are spirit and life. There are some of you who do not believe. . . . This is why I told you that no one can come to me unless it is granted him by the Father."

Jesus knew some of his followers were false professors, that is, they professed faith in Christ, but they didn't possess faith in Christ. They didn't possess faith because the Spirit hadn't given them life, and the Father had not granted that they come to Christ in genuine saving faith.

That is true of many who seem to follow Christ for a while, even for an extended period.

The Parable of the Sower is pointing to this reality. Then, a few verses later in John 6:66, John gives us this important detail: "After this many of his disciples turned back and no longer walked with him." Those who were not given life by the Spirit, who were not granted faith by the Father, went away after following Jesus for a time. This demonstrates that they were never Christians in the first place.

1 John 2:19 says it plainly:

> They went out from us, but they were not of us; for if they had been of us, they would have continued with us. But they went out, that it might become plain that they all are not of us.

That explains all the stories you have about those who walked with God, seemingly, for even a long time, but didn't complete their race. As John says there, they were never one of us or they would never have gone out from us.

Writing of the conclusion of the Sermon on the Mount, where Jesus speaks of two builders and two buildings, many presumptive Christians will be blindsided by their exclusion from the kingdom of Christ, as J. C. Ryle expressed plainly and powerfully:

> The day of judgment will reveal strange things. The hopes of many, who were thought great Christians while they lived, will be utterly confounded. The rottenness of their Christianity will be exposed and put to shame before the whole world. It will then be proved that to be saved means something more than praying the "sinners prayer." We must make a practice of our Christianity as well as a profession.[3]

Do you see how the Parable of the Sower explains the many different responses people, even people in church who seem to be genuine believers, have to the gospel?

Young Christian

It really does. I've noticed also that there are passages in Scripture that seem to portray salvation as a condition. There are several places in Hebrews

---

[3] J. C. Ryle, *Expository Thoughts on the Gospels: Volume 1: Matthew* (Leyland, England: Evangelical Press, 2024), 77.

and in Paul's writings where this seems to be the case. Can we talk about that?

Pastor

We've covered a lot here and have a lot to chew on, so let's take a look at some of those passages next time.

Questions for
Further Reflection

1. Can you think of some real-life examples of people who seem to have come to saving faith in Jesus Christ, but who later walk away?

2. Why does the Parable of the Sower help explain how some will walk with Christ for a season, but ultimately walk away?

3. How does Jesus use that parable to outline four different responses to the gospel? What are those four responses?

4. What New Testament character serves as a major illustration for the "false professor?"

5. What New Testament character serves as a major illustration for the person who remains in the faith even through many temptations, toils, and snares?

6. What does 1 John 2:19 tell us about the issue of apostasy?

CHAPTER 4

Lest We Drift Away from It: What about the Warning Passages? (Part 1)

My crimes are great but don't surpass
Thy power and glory of Thy grace;
Great God, Thy nature hath no bound,
So let thy pardoning love be found.[1]

Young Christian

One of my friends told me a story about a woman he'd led to Christ. She grew strong in the Lord for about two years, attending church regularly, taking part in Bible studies, and giving every sign

---

[1] Isaac Watts, Psalm 51

of a regenerate person who was bearing healthy spiritual fruit. After a couple of years, she began to change. She regularly got drunk. She moved in with a man who was a Buddhist.[2]

Those passages we examined last time seem clear and make sense theologically, but there are other places in Scripture that make it sound like salvation is conditional, as if is based on our obedience. Those passages are kind of scary to me because I'm not perfectly obedient all the time. What I have in mind is several sections of the book of Hebrews, especially Hebrews 6. One of my cousins said that chapter proves that if a Christian falls into sin, they can, as she puts it, "lose out with God" in the end, by which she means lose your salvation. I've read the book of Hebrews, and I've got to admit that her argument seems to hold at least some water.

Pastor
The book of Hebrews can be a sticky wicket if it's not interpreted carefully, and I've heard those Arminian arguments before. Bible scholars refer to those areas in Hebrews as warning passages. According to Tom Schreiner, there are five such

---

2 Tom Schreiner, *Run to Win the Prize: Perseverance in the New Testament* (Wheaton, IL: Crossway, 2010), 16.

warning passages in Hebrews, found in Hebrews 2:1-4, 3:7-4:14, the one you just mentioned which stretches from Hebrews 5:11 through 6:12, and the final two in Hebrews 10:26-31 and 12:25-29. Open your Bible, and we'll look at each of them in turn.

Young Christian

That'll be great, but before we do that, could you explain to me the different views evangelical Christians tend to take with these warning passages, because it seems to me that believers from different denominational backgrounds interpret them differently.

Pastor

Sure, I think that's a good idea. I want to be careful to represent the other views accurately, and this will give me a chance to make sure I do that. Sometimes we can unfairly caricature others' views, particularly if we strongly disagree with what they believe about certain things. There are basically four different views among conservative evangelicals.

First is what I'll call the Arminian view. Some Christians believe Hebrews 6 and the other warning passages are addressed to genuine Christians who, if they violate the warnings, will apostatize and fall away from the faith. We'll continue to call that the Arminian view and that's the one I'm trying to prove unbiblical in our discussion. "If apostasy were not possible, they maintain, then why would the warnings be included? Warnings are superfluous if it is impossible to fall away."[3] Many Methodists, Pentecostals, Free Will Baptists, and some non-denominational churches teach this view.

The second is what is often called the loss of rewards view. Christians who take this approach agree with Arminians that the warning passages are written to genuine believers, but they speak to losing rewards in heaven and not forfeiting eternal life. In the United States, this view has been promoted by the Grace Evangelical Society[4] among others.

Christians and churches that are more Calvinistic in their theology typically hold one of the other two views.

Let's call the third view the "phenomenological view" or what some of the old Christians called the "almost Christian." It's called phe-

3 Ibid., 25.

4 Ibid.

nomenological because the phenomena of their lives make it seems as if they are believers. This argument says warning passages are addressed to unbelievers who are very near to becoming Christians, but, like the first soil in the Parable of the Sower, they fall back and demonstrate that saving faith has not taken root in them. The great Puritan theologian John Owen held this view as does modern-day theologian Wayne Grudem.

The final view, which I'll call the effectual warning view, asserts that the warning passages are written to genuine Christians as means of grace in the hands of God that cause them to continue to persevere in the faith—all the way to the end. God uses the warnings as means to uphold their faith as they run the race of salvation. Many contemporary Calvinists including Tom Schreiner and Ardel Caneday[5] take this approach to the warnings, as does the well-known English Puritan John Bunyan (1628-1688), which he expresses in one of his lesser-known works called *The Heavenly Footman: An Epistle to All the Slothful and Careless People.*

---

5 For a detailed, scholarly examination of this view, see Thomas R. Schreiner and Ardel B. Caneday, *The Race Set Before Us: A Biblical Theology of Perseverance and Assurance* (Downers Grove, IL: InterVarsity Press, 2001).

Young Christian

So which approach is the correct one? Which one do you see is best?

Pastor

I find the effectual warning sign view most consistent with both Scripture and the Christian life. I think the third view is also plausible, so at the risk of sounding like I'm halting between two opinions, I'm going to say the final two are plausible interpretations and applications.

Obviously, you know by now that I reject the Arminian view because the overwhelming witness of Scripture affirms final perseverance for believers. I don't think a loss of rewards doctrine can be sustained because Hebrews never clearly refers to rewards being at stake; it seems clear enough that salvation is on the line in these passages.

The final two views are appealing because both may be argued biblically and both square with Christian experience. There are many unbelievers who sort of get to the one-yard-line with the Lord, but go away, never to return. It then becomes clear that Satan has snatched away the Word, so they didn't believe and weren't saved. As Hebrews 6 says, they have "once been enlightened" and have "tasted the heavenly gift, and have shared in the Holy Spirit, and have tasted the goodness of the word of God and the powers of the age to come" and then have fallen away. They have rejected the only way to salvation even though they experienced a foretaste of it. They've tasted the good things of God, but they have not eaten the full meal. As Matthew Meade (1630-1699), another English Puritan, puts it, they are "almost Christians." He writes this: "A person may have a great deal of knowledge, a great deal of insight; they may understand a lot about God and his will, a lot about Christ and his ways—and still only be almost a Christian."[6] This person is similar to King Agrippa in Acts 26:28, who says after Paul confronts him with the gospel, "Almost thou persuadest me to be a Christian" (KJV). And it's another reason why this whole doctrine is built around the phrase "kept by God."

Young Christian
But you said that you find what you called the effectual warning view a little more convincing?

---

6 Matthew Mead, *The Almost Christian Discovered in Modern English* (Independently published, 2023), 31.

Pastor

I really do think the final two views are valid applications because both things are true. There are some who seem to fall just short of coming all the way to Christ in a salvific way, and God does use means to energize his people to persevere in the faith. The final view, which would be the view I hold if it were illegal to hold more than one view or see only one application for the warning passages (thankfully, it's not) appeals to me because it's like God's warning sign, which is why I've often labeled them God's "effectual warning signs."

Back in 1995, just after my wife and I were married, a strong remnant of Hurricane Opal made it all the way from the Gulf Coast to western North Carolina where we lived. The storm produced torrential rains and severe flooding in the Smoky Mountains, causing numerous mud slides. There was a slide near the town in which we lived that brought the entire side of a mountain down into the valley below. A major two-lane road was perched on that mountainside like a bird's nest, and about 100 yards of the blacktop washed away; it left a gaping hole around 100 feet deep. It happened at night without warning and several vehicles wound up careening into the hole after the road disappeared in front of them. The road department arrived soon and put up road-blocks with huge warning sides on both sides of the newly formed canyon. The signs stopped cars from unwittingly driving off the cliff and into the muck below. Those warning signs kept drivers from injury and death.

I see these warnings in Hebrews and in other places in Scripture functioning the same way. Christians read them and respond to them by continuing to trust in Christ as their Lord and Savior.

Young Christian

That's really helpful. Do you want to look at the individual warnings in Hebrews?

Pastor

Yes, definitely so, but I will try to briefly discuss each one. New Testament scholars don't all agree on how many warning passages there are in Hebrews or where each one begins and ends, so I'm going to use Tom Schreiner's list taken from the New Testament theology class I took with him in seminary and also from his commentary on Hebrews and a couple of books he's written on the issue of perseverance and assurance.

Schreiner lists the warning passages as: Hebrews 2:1-4, 3:7-4:13, 5:11-6:12, 10:26-31, and 12:25-29.[7] There are three issues to be sorted out with these warning passages. First, to whom are the warnings addressed? Second, what is the nature or character of the warning? Third, what is the consequence of failing to heed the warning?[8] Let's look at the first one, Hebrews 2:1-4.

Young Christian

I'm going to open my Bible to these passages. You've taught us to be like the Bereans and check everything against Scripture.

Pastor

I would have it no other way. I'm not infallible, but God's Word cannot err. In Hebrews 2:1-4, I find it interesting that the author includes himself in the admonition: "Therefore, *we* must pay much closer attention to what *we* have heard, lest *we* drive away from it" (v. 1). Obviously, he needs to hear the warning, too, which suggests it is written to confront Christians. He does the

---

7 Schreiner, *Run to Win the Prize*, 41.

8 Ibid.

same thing in the second warning in 3:7-14:13, addressing it to "brothers."

Like many scholars and pastors, I believe Hebrews is a sermon and like all good sermons, this one contains many exhortations, which is what the warning passages are. In 2:1-4, the author is telling listeners that they must pay close attention to the things of the Son, so they do not drift in their faith.[9] Believers must keep their eyes fixed on Jesus, else they might drift away from the only place where salvation may be found. Both phrases have nautical connotations, as in a ship being moored to the shore. The first refers to tying a ship or boat to the dock, the second "drift away" carries the idea of a ship that wasn't tethered to the dock and it floated out of the harbor and drifted into dangerous waters. That's what happens when Christians leave the church, begin to live in unrepentant sin, or reject the orthodox gospel of sacred Scripture. They are set adrift and the current gradually pulls them away from the Christ of the Bible—the only Christ who is mighty to save.

The argument here is from lesser to greater. In Hebrews 1:8-9, the writer tells us that what the angels said in giving the moral law of God

---

9 Robert J. Cara, *Hebrews, a Mentor Commentary* (Ross-Shire, Great Britain: Christian Focus, 2024), 81.

(Deuteronomy 33:2 suggests the angels played a role in the giving of the law) to Moses at Sinai was reliable, but what came through one superior to angels, Jesus, is even more reliable. Jesus attested to his messiahship with various signs, wonders, and miracles. He is reliable; thus, they must fix their faith on him. By doing this, believers will be saved in the end. The apostles were eyewitnesses of what Jesus said and did in his life, ministry, death, and resurrection.

Young Christian

So, you're saying God uses this warning to bring about perseverance? Christians read about what will happen if they neglect Christ and it leads them to continue trusting Christ?

Pastor

Yes, the Holy Spirit indwelling a Christian strengthens them in such a way that they persevere. That is one of the things the Spirit does in us—he causes us to persevere. We do participate in some way in our sanctification, but it is also his work, and our perseverance is entirely a work of God.

Next, let's look at the exhortation in Hebrews 3:7-4:13. Here, the author harkens back to the Old Testament, to the time of Moses Israel was tested in the wilderness, when they hardened their hearts and no longer followed God. That's the warning here. And he goes on to say of that generation of Israelites, "They always go astray in their heart; they have not known my ways" (3:10). He warns believers not to be like them: "Take care, brothers, lest there be in any of you an evil, unbelieving heart, leading you to fall away from the living God. . . . that none of you be hardened by the deceitfulness of sin" (3:12-13). He warns them against hardening their hearts as Israel did when the Israelites were tested in the wilderness. They were unable to enter into God's rest because of unbelief. They didn't lose their salvation, they proved to be unbelievers. This is a warning for believers against deception.

I've known many who walked with the Lord, or it seemed they were his until the skies grew dark in their lives. And they walked away. As Schreiner puts it, "Falling away from the true and living God is an unmitigated disaster, comparable to trying to make it to the top of Mount Everest without proper equipment."[10] Later in chapter 4, the author of Hebrews will speak of a Christ who

---

10 Thomas R. Schreiner, *Commentary on Hebrews* (Nashville: B&H, 2015), 127.

is able to sympathize with our weaknesses, who has been tempted (like Israel) in every way as we are, yet without sin" (4:15). Hebrews 4 concludes by pointing struggling believers to the comfort of all comforts: "Let us then with confidence draw near to the throne of grace, that we may receive mercy and find grace to help in time of need" (4:16).

Young Christian
That's a lot to think about. And there are three more warning passages in Hebrews?

Pastor
Yes. Tell you what, I've given you much to consider in the first two warning passages. Let's begin with Hebrews 6 next time, because that's going to be a longer conversation. We can cover the others as well and briefly outline other warning passages in the New Testament.

Questions for
Further Reflection

1. How many warning passages are there in He-brews? Where are they found?

2. What four views of the warning passages are most common among evangelical Christians? What are the strengths and weaknesses of each?

3. Why is it central to perseverance for a believer to fix his or her eyes on Jesus Christ? What did Christ endure across the entire span of his life and ministry in order that we might be saved and endure to the end?

4. How does the book of Hebrews help us to interpret the Old Testament?

CHAPTER 5

Warning Passages, Part 2

Stand up, my soul, shake off thy fears,
And gird the gospel armour on;
March to the gates of endless joy,
Where they great Captain-Savior's gone.[1]

Young Christian

The warning that really confuses me is the one in Hebrews 6. It sounds like a true Christian can lose their salvation and never get it back. One of my co-workers pointed me to that passage as proof that the Bible teaches salvation can be forfeited. Is he correct?

---

[1] Isaac Watts, "The Christian Warfare"

Pastor

A portion of Hebrews 6 is the Arminian's best proof text, in my opinion, but it doesn't teach final apostasy, unless we are willing to say that once lost, salvation can never be regained. I know many Arminian Christians, but I've not met one who reads it that way—thankfully.

Tom Schreiner points out a major mistake some pastors and scholars make in interpreting Hebrews 6:

> The warnings should be read synoptically, and hence the warnings are mutually illuminating. Many scholars have made the mistake, for instance, of isolating Hebrews 6 from the other warning texts, so that they sink their energies into reading Hebrews 6 alone. Or they inadvertently start reading the warning of Hebrews 6 as if it represents a defection that has already taken place.[2]

I don't believe the Bible is a bipolar book as liberal Protestantism sees it; it either teaches that we cannot forfeit salvation or we can, so if

---

[2] Schreiner, *Run to Win the Prize*, 40.

Hebrews 6 teaches the possibility of final apostasy for true believers, then it contradicts much of what I've already sought to show you from the New Testament—passages such as John 10:28 that clearly depict our salvation as irreversible.

Let's get to the heart of the matter and take a quick look at 6:4-9, which are the verses often debated among evangelicals. We'll take it phrase by phrase:

Once been enlightened (4a). These are people who have had the knowledge of God disclosed to them through the good news of the gospel. They may have even been baptized, for the term for "enlightened" used here was often used as a synonym for Christian baptism in the writings of the early church. In other words, the "enlightenment" spoken of here means the person has heard and has intellectually understood spiritual, biblical truth. It does not mean they accepted or rejected it, believed or disbelieved it.

Tasted the heavenly gift (4b). This could be one of several things. Some see this as participation in the Lord's Supper. Others see it as the Holy Spirit, since the Holy Spirit is spoken of in the New Testament as a gift, but since the Spirit is mentioned in the next phrase, I think this is unlikely. I agree with John MacArthur and believe the gift spoken of here is Christ himself and the salvation he bought. I believe paying close attention to the language here is key: this great gift was only *tasted*; it was not *feasted* upon. The gift of Christ and the gospel was not accepted or lived or treasured, it was only tasted or examined. One of the ways in which the Holy Spirit draws men to Christ is through tasting the Gospel. But, as MacArthur argues, "tasting is not eating."

Shared in the Holy Spirit (4c). The audience here had likely seen the power of the Holy Spirit work in their midst in the congregations with signs and wonders. They had seen the gifts of the Holy Spirit operate in a powerful way, but they had not been indwelt by the Spirit. It is possible to have an association with the Holy Spirit and yet not be saved, not have the Spirit within you. It's not necessary to conclude that regeneration is intended by this phrase.

Tasted the goodness of the Word of God (5). As with the heavenly gifts, they had heard God's utterances and sampled them, tasted them without actually eating them. They had heard the Word of God preached and taught through regular church attendance. They took it all in, possibly with great enthusiasm and appreciation, but they could not say with Jeremiah, "Your words were found, and I ate them and your words became for me a joy and the delight of my heart" (Jer. 15:16). Sadly, many people in this category populate rolls of evangelical churches today.

Tasted the powers of the age to come (5). They had seen the Spirit work through signs and wonders. They had seen him turn sinful hearts to God within the Christian community, but they had not experienced regeneration themselves.

Then have fallen away (6). I believe this is referring to a sustained, committed, hardened rejection of Christ and a departure from the church. Many believe there is a kind of falling away that is irreversible, and it's possible that 1 John 5:16 is referring to this sobering reality. In the same way that salvation is final, a decision to reject Christ as the Savior, if made at a certain level cannot be reversed. This is what is spoken of in 1 John 2:19, "They went out from us, but they were never one of us. . ."

You may even ask: "What if I am worried about losing my salvation or committing the impossible sin?" If you are deeply concerned about this sin, then it is a certain sign that you have not committed it and will not. Satan would prefer that you be lackadaisical about the unpardonable sin than anxious about it; those who are concerned about it will flee to Christ for assurance. That's the last thing Satan wants. The first part of verse 6 really contradicts the Arminian view of assurance of salvation.

Impossible to restore them again to repentance (6a). If the Arminians are correct, then once lost, salvation may never be regained. Arminius himself actually believed this, and I think it is more consistent to think this way, but John Wesley didn't agree. Here's what I think the author is driving at: It is impossible to restore them to repentance because they have rejected the only one who can forgive sins. There is no other place they can go for repentance. Look at the wording: "*Impossible…*" A sobering word indeed. This tells us that rejecting Christ after having encountered him can have a hardening effect that is deadly to our souls.

They are crucifying afresh the Son of God to their own harm and holding him up to contempt. (6b) By renouncing their faith in Christ they declare that Christ's cross is not a holy sacrifice for sins. To reject Christ is to say that he got what he deserved as a criminal and is nothing more than a madman who claimed to be God. Apostates have come to a point where the cross does them no good but instead condemns them as accomplices in Christ's murder. They are holding Christ up to contempt and making a mockery out of his death. When a person does this, in effect he takes up the hammer and nails and drives them into his hands and feet and is alongside those who crucified him, who mocked him like the soldiers who laughed and sneered "He saved others; he cannot save himself" (Mark 15:31). And Christ's sacrificial death cannot be repeated. A believer participates in Christ's death, which is sealed by baptism (Rom. 6:3-4; Col. 2:12), and it cannot be withdrawn and repeated.

Young Christian

Why does the writer then talk about a crop? That seems like it might be an important part of understanding this warning. Is this related somehow to the Parable of the Sower?

Pastor

That's a great insight, because it is very important in understanding this warning. Yes, you do need to think back to our previous discussion about the Parable of the Sower. Agricultural metaphors are found in the Old Testament and New Testament alike, so the writer illustrates his warning against apostasy by setting forth two types of fields in verses 7-8: the productive field and the unproductive field. The author is warning that those who fall away are like the land that does not bear a crop that is useful, that bears thorns and thistles—sagebrush and briars in Deep South terms. The picture is sobering in verse 8: the author says such unfruitful land is near to being cursed and its end is to be burned.

The Old Testament background from Isaiah 5:1-7 speaks of the ground as God's people and Isaiah 55:10-11 calls the Word the rain which falls on God's people. This is the key to properly understanding this passage. Refer back to the four kinds of hearts, the four soils, into which proclamation of the gospel falls: the hard heart (the seed sown along the path), the shallow heart (the seed sown on rocky ground), the strangled heart (the seed sown among the thorns), and the good heart (the seed sown in good soil).

Young Christian
What is the application here for us, then?

Pastor
I think it's at least this: It often takes time to accurately assess a profession of faith. Both Hebrews 6:7-8 and the Parable of the Sower teach us this

vital truth. There is one way to positively identify those who belong to Christ: growth over time. A farmer plants corn, but if he examines the field the morning after he plants it, he would be wrong to conclude that the crop is a failure. Obviously, nothing will have begun to grow in so short a time. But if he comes back in three months after much rain has fallen on the crops and they have received abundant sunshine, then he may see some fruit. It may not be mature yet, but the plant will have germinated and is growing. It takes time and patience. How quick are we to pronounce as a genuine Christian one who "prays the sinner's prayer?" The allegedly converted person goes away and never shows any evidence of being a Christian, yet, when a preacher stands over them at the end of their lives, he pronounces the person to be a citizen of heaven.

Young Christian

It seems this passage might also help diagnose a person's spiritual condition in terms of whether they bear healthy fruit. Isn't that what the writer is driving at in verse 7: "The land that drinks the rain and produces a useful crop" would be a true believer?

Pastor

Yes, for sure. Healthy tomato vines produce nice, ripe tomatoes, and true believers will bear fruit. This is what Jesus said in Matthew 7:18-20, "*A healthy tree cannot bear bad fruit, nor can a diseased tree bear good fruit. Every tree that does not bear good fruit is cut down and thrown into the fire. Thus you will recognize them by their fruits.*"

Young Christian

Must a Christian bear good fruit all the time before you'd consider their profession of faith to be true?

Pastor

That's an important question. We must point out that truly regenerate believers can do terrible things, as King David showed when he committed adultery and murder, as Peter showed when he betrayed our Lord three times. But both showed fruit in genuine, Spirit-wrought repentance.

The historical record of the church has revealed this time and again. A good tree—that is, one truly connected to Christ and having the Holy Spirit at work within—will necessarily go on to bear good fruit. It cannot do otherwise. The bad tree simply lacks the power to bear lasting fruit unto God, however well-watered it may be, however real its second-hand experience of salvation by virtue of affiliation with a local church. Particularly under trial or hardship, it produces only thorns and thistles, and thus it is, as we read here, "worthless and near to being cursed, and its end is to be burned" (Heb. 6:8). It is under God's wrath! In verse 9 the author is certain that better things are true of his audience. Why? Because there is fruit as is clear in 9-10: "Though we speak in this way, yet in your case, beloved, we feel sure of better thigs—*things that belong to salvation*. For God is not unjust as to overlook your work and the love that you have shown for his name in serving the saints, *as you still do*."

Young Christian

Sounds like the writer is certain they are believers. They are being persecuted and are tempted to turn back to Judaism, which is an easier road, but he's encouraging them to persevere. Is that right? And is that what you mean by these warning passages being a means of God's preserving grace in the lives of believers?

Pastor

Yes, and yes. And that's precisely where he goes with 6:11-12, "And we desire each one of you to show the same earnestness to have the full assurance of hope until the end, so that you may not be sluggish, but imitators of those who through faith and patience inherit the promises." He's saying that there is a race to be run, and you must run it. Part of running that race is making sure you're not sluggish in Christian duties and that you look to those who have already persevered in the faith all the way to the end. He picks up on this in Hebrews 11-12, what many call the "hall of faith" which is a spotlighting of Old Testament heroes who lived faithfully for the Lord and graduated to glory. He calls them, in 12:1, a "great cloud of witnesses," who surround those of us still running the race. They are a witness to running the race faithfully, but more than that, they are a witness to the faithfulness of God, who enables us to run our race.

Still, there is a race to be run. Yes, God gives believers the ability to persevere, but there is also a race we must run all the way to the finish line. This is the complementary nature of God's sovereignty and human responsibility we see that runs like twin threads throughout Scripture. Yes, God perseveres us in the faith, but we also must run the race. Both statements are true.

Young Christian
What about Hebrews 10:26-31? It speaks of sinning deliberately: "For if we go on sinning deliberately after receiving the knowledge of the truth, there no longer remains a sacrifice for sins, but a fearful expectation of judgement, and a fury of fire that will consume the adversaries..."

Pastor
That is the fourth of five warning passages in Hebrews. The willful sin here is abandoning one's confession altogether, trampling the Son of God underfoot, treating his blood as unclean, and insulting God's gracious Spirit. This sin is so flagrant because it is willful, premeditated. This is a warning for believers to spur them to holiness and also an exhortation for those who profess faith in Christ but do not really possess eternal life. Those who abandon Christ have nowhere else to turn for forgiveness. Remember, many in John's Gospel walked with Jesus for a time, but when the cost of discipleship was too great, they proved themselves to be false disciples.

There's an argument in Hebrews 6 from lesser to greater: if Israel's abandoning obedience to the moral law of God in the old covenant in exchange for worship of other deities warranted punishment, how much worse will the end be for those who sin boldly and reject Christ, the one true Savior? This is urging believers not to sin boldly, to use a phrase popularly related to Martin Luther's testimony. A genuine believer will heed the warning. But leaving Christ for a life of sin is the path to destruction. In verses 26 and 27 he's saying if we reject Christ after having learning about him and his substitutionary death for sinners, there is nowhere else we can go. All other roads lead to eternal death.

Young Christian
There's one more in Hebrews 12:25-29. That seems to be another argument from lesser to greater.

Pastor
Indeed, it is similar to Hebrews 10. Moses warned from earth and those who rejected him did not escape judgment. Jesus warns from heaven; rejection of his warning will certainly incur God's wrath as well. The threats of God's wrath

here serve as a means of perseverance for the people of God. They hear the sobering message of God's eternal wrath for their sin, and it becomes a means of their continuing in the faith. These two warnings are for us all because I fear that on the day of God's final judgment, there will be some who populate churches who will learn they were never Christians at all. All the warnings here call for close, careful examination by all followers of Christ. Our hearts are easily deceived because we tend to think we are holier than we actually are; we are more sinful than we even know. As we draw closer to Christ, we see that to be true.

Young Christian

Are there warning passages only in Hebrews? Are there others in the New Testament?

Pastor

No, there are warning passages scattered throughout the New Testament. Really, any place you see the important little word "if," you are probably looking at a warning passage. Paul's words in Colossians 1:21-23 are a prime example:

> And you, who once were alienated and hostile in mind, doing evil deeds, he has

now reconciled in his body of flesh by his death in order to present you holy and blameless and above reproach before him, *if indeed you continue in the faith,* stable and steadfast, not shifting from the hope of the gospel that you heard . . .

Let's look at a few in the order they appear, beginning with the Gospels.[3] In Matthew 10:32-33, Jesus warns, "So everyone who acknowledges me before men, I also will acknowledge before my Father who is in heaven, but whoever denies me before men, I also will deny before my Father who is in heaven." Schreiner again helps here:

> Clearly, Jesus speaks to all his disciples here, so the text cannot be confined to those who are almost Christians. The decision facing the disciples is starkly put. Either they acknowledge Jesus before others or they deny him. If they confess him as Lord and Christ, he will acknowledge them as belonging to him before the Father. If, on the other hand, they repudiate

---

[3] I am choosing these warning passages in accord with Tom Schreiner's work, *Run to Win the Prize: Perseverance in the New Testament* (Wheaton, IL: Crossway, 2010).

and deny him, then he will disavow them before the Father. It seems quite clear in the context that the penalty threatened is not merely loss of rewards but final judgment—being excluded from the Father's gracious presence. Such a view is confirmed by the remainder of the discourse, for Jesus also affirms that only "the one who endures to the end will be saved" (Matt. 10:22). Conversely, then, those who fail to continue in the faith will be destroyed.[4]

Next, let's look at John 15:6, "If anyone does not abide in me, he is thrown away like a branch and withers; and the branches are gathered, thrown into the fire, and burned." How does that land on you?

Young Christian
It's a bit frightening. It makes me want to do everything possible to abide in Christ. As you have said, salvation is a sovereign act of God, but there is also a race to be run. Looks like those who do

---

4 Schreiner, *Run to Win the Prize*, 28-29.

not abide in Christ wither up and die. This is another agricultural image from Jesus, isn't it?

Pastor
It is. The idea is that the dead branches who do not abide in Christ, the vine, do not bear fruit and are collected and thrown into the fire. I've already mentioned one warning passage from Paul found in Colossians 1:21-23 above. The warning is in verse 23: ". . . if indeed you continue in the faith." Saving faith is enduring faith, faith anchored in Christ. That's Paul's argument here: there is a race we must run, and those with genuine faith will run it to the end. That warning spurs them on and keeps them from quitting the race when the legs get tired and the knees get weak. There are many other warnings in Paul such as Romans 11:19-22, 1 Corinthians 6:9-11, and Galatians 5:2-4 among others. I'd encourage you to take a closer look at those in your own study time.

Paul's life itself is a testimony to enduring faith as Jonathan Edwards said in a sermon on Philippians 3:17. Paul is not presumptuous and realizes a Christian must finish the race:

> Here you see the apostle is very careful lest he should be a castaway, and denies

his carnal appetites, and mortifies his flesh, for that reason. He did not say, "I am safe, I am sure I shall never be lost; why need I take any further care respecting it (his salvation)?" Many think because they suppose themselves converted, and so safe, that they have nothing to do with the awful threatenings of God's word, and those terrible denunciations of damnation that are contained in it. When they hear them, they hear them as things which belong only to others, and not at all to themselves, as though there were no application of what is revealed in Scripture respecting hell, to the godly. . . . But it was not thus with this holy apostle, who certainly was safe from hell, and as far from a damnable state, as any of us. He looked on himself as still nearly concerned in God's threatenings of eternal damnation, notwithstanding all his hope, and all his eminent holiness, and therefore gave great diligence, that he might avoid eternal damnation.[5]

---

5 From Jonathan Edwards' sermon "The Character of Paul an Example to Christians" as quoted in Schreiner, *Run to Win the Prize*, 33-34.

Young Christian

Edwards is saying that Paul took the warnings of Scripture seriously. So that must have been what Paul was driving at in 1 Corinthians 9:27 when he wrote, "I discipline my body to keep it under control, lest after preaching to others I myself should be disqualified." Is Paul saying that it's possible that he could take God's mercy for granted, preach the Word, and prove to be lost in the end?

Pastor

That's excellent exegesis, because that's exactly what he's saying. There is a race to be run by the believer and the warnings earlier in that letter spur on Paul and keep him from sinful presumptuousness. There have been in the history of the church lost men who preached the very gospel that ultimately condemned them. But Paul, as Edwards said, had no reason to doubt that he was a genuine believer.

There's another warning passage in 2 Peter 1:5-11, where Peter exhorts readers to "make every effort to supplement your faith" with several virtues, a short list of things like self-control, knowledge of God, godliness, brotherly love, and similar fruits. Then he says, "For if these qualities are yours and are increasing, they keep you from being ineffective and unfruitful in the knowledge of our Lord Jesus Christ." At first glance, it seems Peter might be promoting some form of works righteousness, but he isn't. Why not? Because verse 5 makes clear that the fruits are the result of faith.

Then, Peter goes on to warn those who lack these qualities, they are "blind, having forgotten that he was cleansed from former sins." It's a warning clearly written to believers—he calls them "brothers." Peter concludes with another exhortation:

> Therefore, brothers, be all the more diligent to make your calling and election sure, for if you practice these qualities, you will never fall. For in this way there will be richly provided for you an entrance into the eternal kingdom of our Lord and Savior Jesus Christ.

The presence of spiritual fruit such as brotherly love, self-control, and others is a sign that one is truly elect of God. See the logic here: conversion to Christ leads to a transformed life which leads to entrance into God's eternal kingdom.

Therein lies the assurance for the believer: where you see fruit, it is evidence of a healthy root.

Young Christian
Are there other warnings in the New Testament?

Pastor
There are, but our conversation is already long enough. I'll just give you a few texts and let you interact with them: 2 John 7-8, Revelation 2:7, 11, 17, 26; 3:5, 12, and 21. These are just a few more, but they function in the same way as other warning passages we've considered here.[6]

---

6 Ibid.

Questions for
Further Reflection

1. What does Hebrews 6 mean when it speaks of people who have "tasted" the good things of God?

2. How is the agricultural imagery in Hebrews 6 tied to the Parable of the Sower in the Gospels? What would you say about a person who claims to be a follower of Christ but exhibits no fruit at all?

3. What does Jonathan Edwards have to say about finishing the race. What does it mean to say there is a race for the Christian to run? How does that intersect with God's sovereignty in salvation?

4. Look up a few of the warning passages this chapter did not tease out and think through how they apply to perseverance for the believer.

5. What would you say about a longtime pastor who announces that he is leaving the Christian faith? How would you formulate a conclusion based on the biblical teaching we've examined thus far?

CHAPTER 6

If We Can Lose Our Salvation, We Lose the Entire Gospel

Great is Thy faithfulness, O God, my Father;
There is no shadow of turning with Thee.
Thou changest not, Thy compassions they fail not;
As Thou hast been, Thou forever wilt be.[1]

Young Christian

Okay, so evangelical Christians disagree on perseverance and apostasy. Do you think it really matters in the greater scheme of things? Is this something that is secondary to the gospel, a doctrine on which good Christians can disagree with no problem? I mean, it's not heresy or anything is it?

---

[1] Thomas O Chisolm, "Great Is Thy Faithfulness"

Pastor

I believe it's a huge problem. I wouldn't quite put it under the category of heresy like denying the deity of Christ, the Virgin Birth, or the resurrection of Christ, but I would argue that it is a very dangerous teaching. Belief in the possibility of final apostasy for a true believer doesn't mean a person who holds that view isn't saved, but I think it greatly impoverishes their walk with the Lord, which we will get to a little later. For now, I'll say it's a very dangerous teaching for theological and practical reasons. Plus, I think if I could forfeit my salvation, given even the indwelling sin that remains in me, I would. I'll say this: if a genuinely saved person can fall from grace, it makes a mess out of the Christian faith because it undermines other critical doctrines. It's like building a house on sand instead of concrete as Jesus warned at the end of the Sermon on the Mount.

Young Christian

Really? Why? I realize it matters for my own assurance, but why do you see this as such a big deal.

Pastor

It is a massively big deal because the central Christian doctrines are tied together and they stand or fall together. It's like a house of cards; if you re-move one, the whole structure collapses. Let me illustrate it this way, then we'll get to the particu-lar biblical and theological reasoning behind my argument.

One time many years ago, I had a landlord from whom I rented an apartment make me what he called "an offer you can't refuse." I thought, either this man is hiding something about the house he was trying to sell me, or his sales tech-nique has been deeply influenced by the Godfa-ther movies. The "deal" was a dirt-cheap price on a house in one of the best parts of town in Lou-isville, Kentucky. It didn't make sense. Deals like this one never find me.

Soon, I learned why he had stamped a give-away price on the house: the foundation was cracked. In a matter of time, the structure would be compromised, and the house would crumble like my son's Lincoln Log creations. It didn't take me long to say no to this house with a hidden but fatal flaw.

Christian theology is similar: if we remove any of the foundational doctrines—the Trinity, the incarnation, the authority of Scripture, the person and work of Christ, and so on—then the entire building of our faith comes tumbling down. The cardinal doctrines of Christianity stand or fall together. I guess you could say losing perseverance of the saints brings with it serious collateral damage, so I think it is far more dangerous to reject this doctrine than perhaps first meets the eye. Like the rickety house I once nearly bought, rejection of perseverance renders unstable many other critical doctrines that rely on it as a solid foundation. If genuine believers can lose their salvation and be cast away forever, consider these biblical teachings. I will run through them one by one, so you may want to take notes:

Election/Predestination and the Love of God

If God chose his people in Christ before the foundation of the world, is it possible for those same people to then "unchoose" themselves? No matter one's view of election, final apostasy seems to render meaningless Scripture's teaching on God's eternal predestining of a people. If God has a people composed of individuals who are his chosen people, how can Scripture call them his people if, in the end, they are not his people?

In Ephesians, Paul says God predestined his elect in love for adoption as sons. In other words, God set his love on his people before the foundation of the world. God loved us long before we loved him: "In this is love, not that we have loved God but that he loved us and sent his Son to be the propitiation for our sins?" (1 John 4:10). As A. W. Pink put it, "It is because God loves us in Christ, and has done so from everlasting, that the gifts of His love are irrevocable."[2] James 1:17 tells us that there is no change in God. The love of God toward us, which is eternal, indeed makes a change in all who are truly his when that love is "shed abroad in our hearts," but it makes no change in him. He cannot change. Rooted in eternity past, his love for us cannot change. What blessed assurance we have in Jesus! Pink's words are beautiful, powerful, and true:

> Marvelous it is that One so infinitely above us, so inconceivably glorious, should not only notice such worms of the earth, but also set His heart upon them, give His Son for them, send His Spirit to indwell them, and so bear with all their imperfections and waywardness as never to remove His lovingkindness from them. . . . God has so solemnly engaged Himself by covenant, and our sins cannot

---

[2] A. W. Pink, *The Attributes of God*, Kindle edition, location 1613.

make it void. . . . God adds, "Neverthe-
less, My lovingkindness will I not utterly
take from him, nor suffer my faithfulness
to fail. My covenant I will not break" (Ps.
89:31-34).[3]

The Atonement

According to Mark 10:45, Christ gave his life as a
ransom for many. Jesus bore God's wrath that we
deserved so he could buy us back from the curse
of the law. If a ransomed one can be finally lost,
doesn't that then mean that the ransom price paid
was not enough to actually purchase its intended
product—the eternal salvation of God's people?
Final apostasy also seems to undermine the substitutionary nature of the atonement, since Christ
was condemned in the place of his people. This
view would seem to indicate that due to an exer-
cise of their free will some of God's people have
once again fallen under condemnation with their
sins no longer covered by the sacrifice of the sub-
stitute—even though they were once covered
through the blood of Christ.

---

3 Ibid.

Justification by Faith

Justification is a legal declaration that because of faith in Christ's work on the cross, one is no longer guilty before God positionally. Final apostasy seems to undermine God's verdict and re-establish guilty charges against those who were previously exonerated by faith in Christ. This view mangles the foundational Reformation truth of sola fide.

Indwelling (or sealing) of the Holy Spirit

In Ephesians 1:13-14, Paul describes believers as those who have been "sealed with the promised Holy Spirit, who is the guarantee of our inheritance until we acquire possession of it, to the praise of his glory." A doctrine of final apostasy undermines Paul's teaching of the Spirit given as a down payment guaranteeing salvation. If salvation can be lost, then the guarantee is meaningless, as is the down payment.

Union with Christ

In his epistles, Paul often uses a phrase it is easy for us to read over and miss, but it is massively important in our salvation and in this discussion: "in Christ." Usually when he uses that term, Paul is speaking of a believer's union with Christ. This is especially prevalent in Ephesians 1:3-14, where

Paul speaks of the blessing of salvation, beginning several phrases with "In Him" (Eph. 1:11, 13) in the same text where he speaks of believers being "sealed with the promised Holy Spirit, who is the guarantee of our inheritance until we acquire possession of it, to the praise of his glory" (1:13-14). There is nothing in all of creation more safe and secure than the believer who is in Christ because there is a spiritual union between every believer and Christ himself, a union that is unbreakable because of Christ.

Colossians 3:3 speaks powerfully to our union with Christ: "For you have died, and your life is hidden with Christ in God." The believer is inseparably united with Christ, so to be "hidden with Christ in God" means that our new life in the Savior is secure. As John 10:29 tells us, what God has freely given cannot be taken away: "My Father, who has given them to me, is greater than all, and no one is able to snatch them out of the Father's hand."

Remember that passage in John 6 where the people are concerned that Jesus is promoting cannibalism by speaking of his flesh as "true food" and his blood as "true drink?" Jesus is using terms that allude to eating and drinking to illustrate the intimacy of the union between Christ and the believer. It is a spiritual union, sometimes called a "mystical union." John's Gospel will later picture the union as a vine and its branches. In verse 56, Jesus says, "Whoever feeds on my flesh and drinks my blood abides in me, and in in him." That's hardly the language of "iffy" abiding.

R. C. Sproul's illustration is helpful here: "If we are outside of a building, in order to get inside, we must go through a door. Once we make the transition, once we cross the threshold from the outside to the inside, we are inside."[4] Bryan Chapell points out that our union with Christ has implications for us, past, present, and future, an insight he rightly sees in Colossians 3:

> In the past, we have been raised with Christ (Col. 3:1) . . . In the present, our lives are hidden with Christ in God (v. 3) . . . In the future, as a result of these past and present realities, when the Savior who is our life appears, we will have the privilege of appearing with Christ in glory (v. 4). There is no 'if, and, or but' here. Rather, there is the glorious assur-

---

[4] R. C. Sproul, *Everyone's a Theologian: An Introduction to Systematic Theology* (Sanford, FL: Reformation Trust, 2014), Kindle edition, Location 3368.

ance that, despite our sin, those who entrust their lives to the Savior are secure in his love.[5]

In a letter to one of his parishioners, John Newton said it better than I ever could: "But faith, uniting us to Christ, fixes us upon a sure foundation, the Rock of ages, where we stand immovable, though storms and floods unite their force against us."[6]

The Promises of God

In John 10, Jesus said, "My sheep hear my voice, I know them, and they follow me. I give them eternal life, and they will never perish and no one will snatch them out of my hand . . . and no one is able to snatch them out of my Father's hand." Also, Philippians 1:6 promises that God will complete the work he begins in his people: "And I am sure of this, that he who began a good work in you will bring it to completion at the day of Jesus Christ." And there is the glorious passage in Romans 8:31-39 promises that nothing can

5 Bryan Chapell, *Holiness by Grace: Delighting in the Joy That Is Our Strength* (Wheaton, IL: Crossway, 2001), Kindle edition, location 2297.

6 John Newton: "Letter XXVIII," in *The Works of John Owen* (Edinburgh: Banner of Truth, 2015), 1:227.

separate the believer from the love of God, which we looked at in a little more depth earlier in our conversation.

But how comforting are these promises if we can, as some argue, remove ourselves from Christ's hand or circumvent the work God has begun in us? In what way to they remain as promises? If these promises are not true, doesn't that undermine the very Word of God? Can we trust a God who is unable to keep his promises from being undone by the power of human choice? No, we couldn't. But God isn't that way. Paul told the Corinthians, "All the promises of God in Him (in Christ) are yes and amen, to the glory of God" (2 Cor. 1:20).

This brings me to another unbreakable part of God's work: his love, which he binds to us by covenant.

God's Covenant with His People
Theologians have rightly called covenants the skeleton of the Bible. God makes a covenant with his people, one he knows they will break, but he will never break. God relates to his people through covenants. O. Palmer Robertson defines a covenant as "a bond in blood sovereignly ad-

ministered."[7] Our salvation and our security are based on God's faithfulness as a covenant keeper. Yes, we will break the covenant by sinning against God, but he will not break it. In the Old Testaments, God made covenants with Noah, Abraham, Moses, David, and others, all part of the Old Covenant that foreshadowed the New Covenant with Jesus Christ the sacrifice and surety that ratified the covenant with us. Some theologians see a covenant of redemption, a covenant of works, and a covenant of grace in Scripture, with all the other covenants functioning as sub-covenants.

The covenant with Abraham in Genesis 15 is perhaps the most odd but clearest in demonstrating God's unbreakable commitment to his people. There, God promises to give Abraham a child and make him into a mighty nation. Abraham believed the Lord and was declared righteous through the instrument of his faith. After this declaration of Abraham's justification before God, the Lord ratifies the divine promise by passing through animals that have been cut up, literally "cutting a covenant" in Hebrew. This act is God's way of placing an oath upon himself

---

7 O. Palmer Robertson, *The Christ of the Covenants* (Phillipsburg, NJ: P&R, 1980), 4.

that he would be torn to shreds like the animals should he fail to keep his promises (Jer. 34:18-20). Of course, that's exactly what happens at Calvary: Jesus is torn apart, not because he broke the covenant, but because we did. He absorbs the divine wrath our sins deserve—that's how committed God is to his people. A man who was not guilty of any sin—Jesus, the second Adam—died for his guilty people, all who came from the first Adam, the original sinner.

Marriage is a covenant relationship between a man and a woman that is ratified before God and man to be permanent, just like the covenants of Scripture. God keeps the covenant because we cannot. Our security, our perseverance is guaranteed by God's covenant faithfulness, not ours. We cannot lose it because an unchanging and eternal God protects it.

Those who hold to the possibility of final apostasy undermine Scripture's teaching on the covenant faithfulness and love of God. One of the attributes of God is his truthfulness: God cannot lie (Num. 23:19; Rom. 3:4; Heb. 6:18) and his veracity is promissory in that he is the faithful God who always keeps covenant and steadfast love (Deut. 7:9; 1 Cor. 1:9).

Intercessory Work of Christ

If Christ lives to intercede for us as Hebrews and Romans 8 contend and as John 17 and Luke 22 demonstrate, then in what meaningful way can we trust his prayers if he does not get what he prays for?

If Christ prays that we will be kept as he does in John 17 and those prayers are frustrated, then it would seem to undermine both his intercessory work and his perfections. That would mean that Christ prays and then hopes his prayers will be answered and that we will remain in the faith. But since Christ is perfectly righteous, as he is praying for us at the right hand of God, he gets that for which he asks. Can you imagine the Lord praying to the Father and having his prayers rejected because man's ability to resist grace is too strong?

Young Christian

That sounds a little scandalous to me.

Pastor

Indeed. If genuine Christians can be lost in the end, it also undermines God's covenant faithfulness. Look at Hebrews 7:24-25, and this, to me, is the clincher. Speaking of Christ being the final high priest, the fulfillment of the high priestly office so vital to old covenant worship, the author Hebrews writes, "but he holds his priesthood permanently, because he continues forever. Consequently, he is able to save to the uttermost those who draw near to God through him, since he always livers to make intercession for them." If a believer can forfeit his salvation, then this passage makes no sense whatsoever. As long as Christ is able to intercede for us, we will remain saved, which is, of course, for all eternity.

Young Christian

I see. Jesus is torn apart on the cross, just like the animals. Jesus is our final high priest. That really helps me to put my Bible together. I cannot see why some Christians believe you can lose your salvation given that it's all dependent on the work of Christ. His ongoing intercession seems to render clear a believer's security.

Pastor

Exactly, and all this is good news. God does it all. I think the Arminian position unwittingly grants man more power than Scripture gives him. God is the one taking the punishment in the place of the covenant-breakers. Fundamentally, the covenant represents the basic structure of the relationship which God has established with man. We usually think of a covenant as an agreement between two equals, similar to a contract, and it is that, but in God's Word, a covenant is not usually an agreement between two equals, and it is certainly not in the covenant God makes with man. The covenants God made with man are modeled after the Suzerain-vassal treaties of the ancient Near East. Those covenants were made between a king and a nation he had conquered. There was no negotiation. So it is with God's covenants with us.

In biblical times, covenants were ratified in blood, which is what God was doing in Genesis 15 with Abraham in that odd-seeming ceremony. This should be beginning to sound familiar to you.

Young Christian

It definitely does. It makes sense of how bloody the Bible is across the entire book.

Pastor

It is a blood-stained book for sure, but that's a good thing. The covenant ceremony with Abraham was a foreshadowing of what God would do to redeem covenant breakers finally and fully through the death of the Messiah who was to come. It was God who would keep the covenant. The idea of the covenant, which was God's idea, is important in understanding that salvation is the work of God alone. He saves us and keeps us saved.

God's promise of redemption in the Old Testament sits at the heart of the new covenant. God has not only promised to redeem all who put their trust in Christ, but has sealed and confirmed that promise with a most holy vow. God has pledged himself to our full redemption. He says this clearly in Jeremiah 31 in speaking of the new covenant, where he compares his promise to the enduring order of the heavenly bodies he's created:

> Thus says the LORD,
> who gives the sun for light by day
> and the fixed order of the moon and the
>   stars for the light by night,
> who stirs up the sea so that its waves
>   roar—
> the LORD of hosts is his name:
> "If this fixed order departs
> from before me, declares the LORD,
> then shall the offspring of Israel cease
> from being a nation before me forever."

111

> Thus says the LORD:
> "If the heavens above can be measured,
> and the foundations of the earth below
>   can be explored,
> then I will cast off all the offspring
>   of Israel
> for all that they have done,
> declares the LORD." (Jer. 31:35-37)

Our salvation is not dependent on us, but on God and his faithfulness. God is not like sinful earthly fathers who sometimes walk out on their families in disgust. A sinner's final salvation is as certain as the Lord's faithfulness to the covenant is certain. Though we don't have time in our conversation for it, the entire book of Hebrews unpacks this for us.

Young Christian

You've summarized the gospel as existing in the *Five Solas* of the Reformation. Doesn't the possibility of final apostasy run contrary to the teaching of those doctrines?

Pastor

No doubt. If we can lose our salvation, then we lose the five *solas* that summarize evangelical teaching out of the Reformation, doctrines that stood at the center of issues the reformers had with the Roman Catholic Church. Ask me about that again in a minute because I want to say this first: final apostasy is really more akin to Roman Catholic teaching than evangelical belief.

Young Christian
Really? What does it have to do with the Reformation?

Pastor
That's a great question, and even more insightful than you may realize. First, let me deal with what it has to do with the Reformation and Roman Catholicism. Sometimes it helps to take at the roots of a long-standing theological debate. Arminianism and the doctrine of falling away didn't begin with John Wesley. It goes back to a post-Reformation figure names Jacob Arminius. When people talk about the debate between Calvinism and Arminianism, few probably know that Jacob Arminius (1560-1609) was a Dutch pastor and professor whose theological training had been thoroughly Calvinistic. He studied in

Geneva under Calvin's successor, Theodore Beza.[8] Arminius later rejected Calvin's understanding of predestination and also perseverance of the saints.

After Arminius died, some of his followers in 1610 published the five articles of the Remonstrants as a challenge to the Calvinistic doctrines of sin and salvation. Dutch Reformed church leaders convened the Synod of Dort in 1618 to refute what they saw as the errors of Arminianism and published what today we call the Five Points of Calvinism.

The fifth point of the so-called TULIP acronym stands for perseverance of the saints. Later in the 18th century, John Wesley (1703-1791) popularized Arminian theology in founding Methodism, embracing the possibility of falling away for a genuine believer. Wesley's version differs slightly than that of Arminius because Wesley coupled with his doctrine of perfection, arguing that it is possible for a believer to live above known sin. Wesley's version of apostasy is popular today among Pentecostal and charismatic Christians, but Arminius is more or less the fountainhead of the doctrine of final apostasy among evangelicals,

---

8 Justo Gonzalez, *The Story of Christianity, Volume 2: The Reformation to the Present Day* (New York: HarperOne, 2010), 229.

at least as a popularizing agent through his followers in framing the Remonstrants.

Young Christian

That is helpful. I was only aware of Wesley. You said a belief that salvation can be lost has more in common with Roman Catholic doctrine than evangelical Christianity? I'm not sure I understand that or agree with it.

Pastor

The Roman Catholic Church teaches that people can and do lose their salvation. If a person commits a mortal sin, such sin kills the grace of justification that inhabits the soul. If he dies before being restored to a state of grace via the sacrament of penance, he will go to hell. A few years ago, I met a man who was a member of an Arminian denomination's church who said he'd lost his salvation four or five times. Each time he had repented and was saved again, he said. This man was a professed evangelical, but his understanding of perseverance was very Roman Catholic.

Young Christian

So, there are evangelicals who believe in mortal sins?

Pastor

No and yes. I use that with contradictory language intentionally. I've never met an evangelical Arminian who says he or she believes in mortal sins in the same way Roman Catholics do, but practically speaking, they do. I met another man at a conference who said he'd recently returned to the Lord after having backslidden away from Christ. He had told several lies and lusted, which he said led to his losing his salvation. He also told me that looking at pornography had cost him his salvation another time. He had repented on each occasion, so he was saved a second and third time.

Young Christian

What do you make of that?

Pastor

I think it's confusing justification with sanctification, which sits at the heart of Roman Catholicism's faulty understanding of perseverance. I'm by no means saying that telling lies, lusting or looking at pornography are not sinful and destructive, those things certainly are sinful and dangerous behaviors. But if a person repents and turns from such sinful pursuits after having made a credible profession of faith, it's not salvation but a part of sanctification. Roman Catholics and evangelicals differ profoundly on the doctrine of final perseverance and an associated teaching that is vital to daily Christian living—assurance of salvation. In his book on Roman Catholic theology, friend Greg Allison summarizes the differences this way, and I only give you this to show that Arminian evangelicals who hold to the possibility that a true Christian can be lost in the end are similar to Roman Catholicism on this point:

> The Catholic positions consider grace to be resistible and faith to be a virtue that can be lost. Thus, the Catholic faithful may forfeit the salvation they once enjoyed. Living under this dark shadow, they deny assurance of salvation. The Catholic view is based on several points. One is that mortal sin results in the loss of grace, which can only be recovered by the sacrament of penance and reconciliation. Should the Catholic faithful commit mortal sin and not avail themselves of grace through this sacrament, they will go to hell. A second support is the Catholic view of human freedom. Possessing libertarian free will, the Catholic faithful may

resist the grace of God, lose their faith, and forget their salvation. And there are no causal factors, including divine intervention and provision of grace, that can decisively stop such a drift away from God. A third point is the Catholic view of justification. As a divine-human cooperative process, if the Catholic faithful do not continue to collaborate and progress in holiness, they will not persevere.[9]

You see how similarly some evangelicals are to Roman Catholicism on perseverance and assurance? Now, Catholics and evangelicals do share common beliefs on some important doctrinal matters such as the Trinity and the Resurrection of Jesus, so that doesn't automatically mean they are wrong about perseverance, but their doctrines here are similar. In fact, I once asked an Arminian relative whether a person would be saved if they told a lie and then died in a car wreck without repenting. Without hesitation, they said "yes." So, Arminians have their list of mortal sins, too.

---

[9] Gregg Allison, *40 Questions about Roman Catholicism* (Grand Rapids: Kregel Academic, 2021), 247.

Young Christian

I've been studying about the five *solas* of the Reformation. You know, the summary of the Reformation's teaching on salvation that I've heard you reference from the pulpit. If memory serves, the word "*sola*" is Latin for "alone," so the *solas* are *sola fide*, *sola gratia*, *solo Christos*, *sola Scriptura*, and *soli deo gloria*, meaning we are saved by faith alone (*sola fide*) through grace alone (*sola gratia*) in Christ alone (*solo Christos*) as revealed in Scripture alone (*sola Scriptura*) to the glory of God alone (*soli deo gloria*). You said a denial of perseverance or security undermines the five *solas*. Help me understand how that's true.

Pastor

Well, first, you are an excellent student as you remember all five with spot-on accuracy. Nicely done! The Arminian view of eternal security or perhaps we should call it "eternal insecurity," rips out the heart of the *solas*. Take *sola fide*; if God saves us and then we must persevere in our own strength, then salvation is by faith plus works. If we accomplish even one percent of our salvation in our own strength, then it is no longer grace, so say goodbye to *sola gratia* and *solo Christos*, because it is grace plus our own strength and Christ plus our own strength.

What I'm saying is this: if we lose the "*sola*" part of the *solas*, we undermine completely the critical part of those precious doctrines. And, of course, if we achieve even one percent of our final salvation, then one percent of the glory goes to our strength, so farewell *soli deo gloria*, which is perhaps the most scandalous of all. God is glorified in the salvation of sinners from the effectual call and new birth to sanctification and final perseverance.

Young Christian

So, you're saying that the core doctrines of Christianity are like a chain and are all linked together.

Pastor

That's exactly what I'm saying. If you lose one, you lose them all. Perseverance/preservation is a vital doctrine. No, it's not heresy to deny it, but I would argue that it's close to heresy because it undermines so much else that lies at the heart of the gospel. As I said earlier, at best I would categorize the Arminian denial of perseverance as dangerous teaching, not only for the disruptive impact it has on Christian theology, but perhaps worst of all, for the practical impact is has on believers. It absolutely kills a Christian's assurance of salvation. Let's discuss that and other practical implications in our next conversation.

Questions for
Further Reflection

1. Is it true that the doctrines of Christianity stand or fall together? Why can't we just read biblical passages and Christian doctrines in isolation from others?

2. The pastor argues that the possibility of final apostasy for a genuine believer undermines the intercessory work of Christ. Why?

3. What other doctrines are completely changed and even overturned if final apostasy were possible for a true believer?

4. What are the *Five Solas* of the Reformation and what do they have to do with perseverance of the saints?

5. Compare and contrast the Reformation view of perseverance with that of Roman Catholicism. How is the Wesleyan view similar to that of Roman Catholics? Why does the pastor view that as a problem?

6. Why does the pastor argue that the possibility of final apostasy undermines the covenants of Scripture?

CHAPTER 7

No Security, No Assurance: How Do I Run the Race?

Where God begins His gracious work,
That work He will complete,
For round the objects of His love,
All power and mercy meet.[1]

"There are two points in religion on which the teaching of the Bible is very plain and distinct. One of these is the fearful danger of the ungodly; the other is the perfect safety of the righteous."[2]

---

[1] Albert Midlane, "Final Perseverance"

[2] J. C. Ryle, *Old Paths* (Cambridge: James Clarke & Co., 1977), 476.

Young Christian

We've been talking about the doctrine itself, but this seems to be an extremely practical issue. If I can lose my salvation, then I don't really have much assurance of salvation because, as you've said, I'm afraid if I could forfeit eternal life, I would.

Pastor

It *is* deeply practical because it undermines a Christian's assurance that he or she is truly born again and bound for heaven. I recently spoke with a person who strongly disagrees with perseverance and she admitted that sometimes she lays awake at night hoping she hasn't committed so much sin that she's not going to make it to heaven. This was a lady whose life has been built around her evangelical church for decades, whose life is full of spiritual fruit, who has walked with the Lord for more than 60 years. Yet, because she believes in the importance of final apostasy, she has very little assurance.

Young Christian

Doesn't that also mean that God saves you, but then it's up to you to keep yourself saved? Where is that found in the Bible?

Pastor

It is not found in the Bible. And I asked that lady: How many sins must you commit to forfeit your salvation? Which sins must you commit? What does the Bible say about that?

Young Christian

The Bible says nothing about that. And am I correct in saying there is not an example in Scripture of a person falling away?

Pastor

Yes, that is correct. It really undermines the power and promises of God when we insinuate that he is not powerful enough to keep us saved. If we can walk away, then that puts the power in our corner.

Young Christian

Why do you think there's so much confusion and outright disagreement among Christians about this doctrine?

Pastor

I believe the misunderstanding lies in two things: First, many Christians don't understand that, while God is sovereign in salvation, there is a race the Christian must run and you must run it all the way to the end. But here's the good news: it is a race that is energized by God's grace. Second, I think there's a misunderstanding of sanctification among some believers. Many seem to have a view of sanctification similar to that of Roman Catholicism in which they collapse together sanctification and justification. We've already dealt with the second misunderstanding earlier when we discussed the way in which final apostasy, if true, undermines the biblical understanding of justification as a legal declaration of not guilty before the court of heaven.

Young Christian
Okay, but can you explain the first misunderstanding a bit more. This seems to be where rubber and road meet as far as this being such a practical matter.

Pastor
Of course. I want our discussion to be thorough without being academic. Hebrews 12:1 puts it succinctly: "Therefore, since we are surrounded by so great a cloud of witnesses, let us lay aside every weight, and sin which clings so closely and let us run with endurance the race that is set be-

fore us . . ." Verse two tells us how to run the race, but let's first look at the reality of the marathon every Christian must run. We'll look at the practicality of verse 2 later. Paul's writings are ripe with athletic imagery describing the race.

Paul in 1 Corinthians 9:24-27 uses the runner metaphor as a well as boxing imagery to show the necessity of running the race.

> Do you not know that in a race all the runners run, but only one receives the prize? So run that you may obtain it. Every athlete exercises self-control in all things. They do it to receive a perishable wreath, but we an imperishable. So, I do not run aimlessly; I do not box as one beating the air. But I discipline my body and keep it under control, lest after preaching to others I myself should be disqualified.

In 2 Tim. 4:6-8, the Spirit-inspired apostle writes,

> *For I am already being poured out as a drink offering, and the time of my departure has come. I have fought the good*

fight, I have finished the race, I have kept the faith. Henceforth there is laid up for me the crown of righteousness, which the Lord, the righteous judge, will award to me on that day, and not only to me but also to all who have loved his appearing.

Similarly, in Philippians 3:12-14, he puts it this way:

Not that I have already obtained this or am already perfect, but I press on to make it my own, because Christ Jesus has made me his own. Brothers, I do not consider that I have made it my own. But one thing I do: forgetting what lies behind and straining forward to what lies ahead, I press on toward the goal for the prize of the upward call of God in Christ Jesus.

Young Christian
This race sounds more like a marathon than a sprint. Those verses seem to be saying there is a long and rigorous race that a Christan must run, one that may last until life on earth is complete.

Pastor

That's exactly the writer of Hebrews and Paul's point and that's my point. Salvation is by grace alone, and yet no one is saved without perseverance. Theologian John Murray helpfully explains: "We do not attain to the prize of the high calling of God in Christ automatically. Perseverance means the engagement of our persons in the most intense and concentrated devotion to those means which God has ordained for the achievement of his saving purpose."

A couple of things to note, and these things are of comfort. First, it is not your course. You are running "the race set before you." And, second, as you alluded, the race is a marathon, not a sprint. Back in Hebrews 10, the author speaks of the Christian's need for endurance. Later in chapter 12, he encourages the believer to consider the way Christ endured the cross, admonishing the reader, "so that you may not grow weary or faint-hearted" (12:3b) and later, "Therefore, lift your drooping hands and strengthen your weak knees, and make straight paths for your feet so that what is lame may not be put out of joint but rather healed" (12:12-13). The journey is going to be wearisome, the road paved with things that will injure your knees and even put them out of joint.

In other words, the Christian life will be both delightful and difficult, glorious and grinding.

Young Christian

But then he tells us how to endure? Is that what's happening in verse 2?

Pastor

Yes, it certainly is. But he began in verse 1, telling readers to "lay aside every weight, and sin that clings so closely," and then writes verse 2, "looking to Jesus, the founder and perfecter of our faith, who for the joy that was set before him endured the cross, despising the shame, and is seated at the right hand of the throne of God."

We endure by killing sin every day. We endure by laying aside anything—any habit or love relationship or hobby or food or sinful lifestyle choice or career ambitions or anything else—that keeps us from running with speed and deft. Ancient Greek Olympic runners trained with weights tied to them and wore long, heavy clothes to make their body lean—"hindrances"—but then stripped off all their garments and ran in the nude. That's the metaphor here. Anything that slows us down in running hard after Christ must be discarded.

Hindrances weigh us down, but sin tangles our feet, bringing us down to the ground. Look at all the men we've seen disqualified from ministry over the past few years because of various sins—adultery, anger, misuse of authority, sexual and physical abuse. And the list goes on and on. Satan deceived them. They didn't deal with indwelling sin and it killed them.

In other words, as the great Puritan theologian John Owen put it, Be killing sin or sin will be killing you. Look how the writer puts it: "the sin that clings to closely." His point is that sin sticks to us. It entangles us. It tackles us to the ground and takes away our ability to run the race.

We take sin lightly to our peril. Sin leads us off the path altogether and sends us running in a different direction as if we are intoxicated by the world. We must be wise regarding sin, daily seeking God's grace to be free from the sins we know about, while shunning the temptations to sin that fly around us every moment. And we keep our eyes fixed on the Savior.

Young Christian

How exactly do we keep our eyes fixed on the Savior? I mean, practically, in the full-court press of everyday life, how can we keep our eyes on Him? If there is a race to be run, how should I run it?

Pastor

I've already alluded to a Christian's first priority and that's to be busy killing sin. Romans 8:13 says, ". . . but if by the Spirit you put to death the deeds of the body, you will live." You must deal with the old man, asking God to put off his deeds, and be praying that God will put on the new man you are becoming in Christ. When we come to Christ, there is a death in us, a slaying of the old man who was captive to sin and death. In Colossians 3:8-10 we are reminded that we once walked captive to the world, the flesh, and the devil, "But now you must put them all away: anger, wrath, malice, slander, and obscene talk from your mouth." Instead, he goes on to say, ". . . you have put off the old self with its practices and have put on the new self, which is being renewed in knowledge after the image of its creator."

Sin was the garment we once wore, but now we are clothed in the righteousness of Christ. He has taken off our old, sin-stained garments and has fitted us with the spotless robes of Christ's righteousness we have obtained by faith in Him.

In Colossians 3:12-14, Paul then goes on to exhort believers:

> Put on then, as God's chosen ones, holy and beloved, compassionate hearts, kindness, humility, meekness, and patience, bearing with one another and, if one has a complaint against another, forgiving each other; as the Lord has forgiven you, so you must also forgive. And above all these put on love, which binds everything together in perfect harmony.

Young Christian

So, in putting off sin, we are also to put on righteous living in the things listed there, which is basically a summary of the fruit of the spirit?

Pastor

Indeed. If you are bearing fruit for righteousness and growing like a healthy tree, then, as the psalmist puts it in Psalm 1, you will "bear fruit in season and your leaf will not wither." Peter says something similar: "Be all the more diligent to make your calling and election sure, for if you practice these qualities you will never fail" (2 Pet. 1:10), speaking of those who seek the fruit of the

Holy Spirit in their lives. As you are transformed, you will have assurance because it will be clear that these things are in you and are increasing.

Young Christian
How do I bear fruit? I can't do it in my own efforts.

Pastor
Paul gets at that a little further on in Colossians 3:16, "Let the word of Christ dwell in you richly, teaching and admonishing one another in all wisdom. . ." As you read, meditate on, and memorize God's Word—"hiding it in your heart so I might not sin against you," as the psalmist puts it (Ps. 119:11)—you will grow and mature in your knowledge of God, your knowledge of yourself, the grace of Christ and your daily reliance upon God, maturity and holiness, along with assurance of salvation, will come.

You do this through what are often called the "ordinary means of grace," which are anything but ordinary. God has invested extraordinary transforming grace in these so-called "ordinary means of grace," things faithful membership and participation in a doctrinally sound local church body, fellowship there with other believers, daily

Scripture reading and meditation, daily prayer, evangelism, serving others, suffering for Christ's sake, and things like that. Give yourself to those things and perseverance will come as naturally as breathing. God doesn't accomplish his ends without using means and these are among the means he uses to cause his redeemed people to run the race with endurance all the way to the end. All this comes to the person who looks to Christ for salvation and then keeps on looking to Him through His Word for a lifetime. J. C. Ryle had some memorable things to say about this truth:

> I wish to caution you most strongly against losing sight of the root of the whole matter—a simple faith in the Lord Jesus Christ. . . . some think of their own endeavours after holiness are to make up their title to salvation; some think that when they come to Christ, their sins past alone are forgiven, and for the time to come they must depend on themselves. Alas! there always have been mistakes upon this point: men toil and labour after peace with God as if their own exertions would give them a right to lay hold on Christ, and when they find themselves far

short of the Bible standard, they mourn
and grieve and will not be comforted;
and all because they will not see that in
the matter of forgiveness, in the matter of
justification in the sight of God, it is not
doing which is required, but believing; it
is not working, but trusting; it is not perfect obedience, but humble faith.[3]

Young Christian

Wait, did you say something about suffering? Is
that really a means of grace for the Christian?

Pastor

Yes, I did say that. Acts 14:22 tells us, ". . . through
many tribulations we must enter the kingdom of
God." Those are Paul's words. Scarcely has any
minister in the history of the church suffered
more profoundly for the sake of Christ than the
apostle Paul. The entirety of 2 Corinthians chron-
icles all that Paul went through to proclaim the
gospel of Jesus Christ as the church's first foreign
missionary. And yet, he calls it "momentary light
affliction that is producing in us a weight of glory
far beyond all compare. . ." How? He goes on to

---

[3] J. C. Ryle, *The Christian Race and Other Sermons* (Light by
Design, 2020), Kindle edition, loc. 1898.

tell us: ". . . looking to the things that are seen, not to the things that are unseen, for the things that are seen are temporal, but the things that are unseen are eternal" (2 Cor. 4:17-18).

Young Christian

How does suffering promote perseverance? Wouldn't that frustrate a believer and tempt them to walk away from the faith? I saw a preacher on television who said God's children are the king's kids and as such should live like the king's kids with perfect health, full bank accounts, big hous- es, and fancy cars. Isn't the Bible here saying the opposite?

Pastor

It absolutely is saying the opposite. What you are describing sounds like what is often called the health and wealth or prosperity gospel. That is a dangerous and unbiblical teaching, what Luther would call "theology from below," a "theology of glory" or far worse—all of which would be war- ranted.

No, we live in a fallen world that is captive to sin, suffering, and death. Turning to Christ does not make one immune to that. Otherwise, we'd have the biggest revival in human history if becoming a Christian guaranteed perfect health and much wealth. Actually, the promises of God are far better with incalculable riches laid up in our inheritance in heaven and future health that is perfect that will enable us to live forever with Christ. The blessings of the true gospel are far greater than the false "this-world" promises of the so-called health and wealth gospel. That's what Paul is driving at in 2 Corinthians 4:17-18. Our best life is not now, but later. The things of God we cannot see are far superior to the things in this world, including money and fame, that we can see.

For the Christian, suffering at the hands of a fallen world or suffering because of our commitment to Christ is a blessing the non-Christian could never understand. Again, Paul tells us about it clearly in Romans 5:3-5:

> We rejoice in our sufferings, knowing that suffering produces endurance, and endurance produces character, and character produces hope, and hope does not put us to shame, because God's love has been poured into our hearts through the Holy Spirit who has been given to us.

Suffering takes our eyes off of this fallen world and focuses us on the perfect world that is to come—where there will be no affliction, no pain, no ambulances, no hospitals, no funeral homes, no cancer, no broken homes. Adversity causes us to cling to Christ and that's part of the way we persevere. As Jonathan Edwards famously said, suffering stamps eternity on our eyeballs.

So, God causes us to persevere in the race, but we also must run. I love the way the old Puritan preacher John Bunyan, author of *Pilgrim's Progress*, put it:

> Arise man, be slothful no longer; set foot, and heart, and all into the way of God, and run, the crown is at the end of the race; there also standeth the loving for-runner, even Jesus, who hath prepared heavenly provision to make thy soul welcome, and he will give it to thee with a willinger heart than ever thou canst desire of him. O therefore do not delay the time any longer, but put into practice the words of the men of Dan to their brethren, after they had seen the goodness of the land of Canaan. . . . Be not slothful to go, and to enter to possess the land. I

wish our souls may meet with comfort at the journey's end.[4]

Young Christian

Perseverance sure does seem like an important doctrine. Why do you think some Christians are so stringently opposed to something that is so clearly taught in the Bible?

Pastor

I think it's because it hasn't been very well taught by some evangelical teachers. It's often called "once saved, always saved," which is true, but I think perseverance of the saints or preservation of the saints is more biblically accurate. For example, one book argues that once a person comes to know Christ, they could immediately join a cult but would still go to heaven. That's not how the Bible teaches the doctrine, and I can understand why some would object to that. Other Christians say it undermines holy living. In other words, they'd say, if you can't lose your salvation, then what would compel you to obey God's com-

---

4 John Bunyan, *The Heavenly Footman* in *The Works of John Bunyan, Vol. 3*, George Offor, ed. (Carlisle, PA: Banner of Truth, 1999), 380.

mandments. Since you can't lose it, you can live any way you want to and still go to heaven.

Thus, I think it's important to say what perseverance is not because I think that's where Arminians have some concerns about what more Reformation-minded Christians believe about it. The late James Montgomery Boice is especially helpful here:

1. "Perseverance does not mean that Christians are free of all spiritual danger just because they are Christians. On the contrary, their danger is even greater, for the world and the devil will be active opponents for them."[5]

2. "It does not mean that Christians are free from falling into sin just because they are Christians."[6] hose who hold to final apostasy tend to veer—unintentionally, I think—into arguing for an unbiblical perfectionism, which is the notion that it is possible for a Christian to live above "known" sin. John

---

[5] James Montgomery Boice, *Foundations of the Christian Faith* (Downers Grove, IL: IVP Academic, 1992), 532.

[6] Ibid.

Wesley and his followers taught this.

Boice gives some powerful, and maybe a bit shocking, biblical illustrations that true believers will continue to battle sin so long as they are on this earth. "Noah fell into drunkenness. Abraham lied twice about his wife Sarah, saying she was his sister, and thus risking her honor to save his own skin. Lot chose Sodom. Jacob cheated his brother Esau and deceived his father Isaac. David committed adultery with Bathsheba, and then tried to cover it up by having her husband, Uriah, killed. In Gethsemane, the disciples abandoned Jesus to protect their own lives. Paul and Barnabas fought over John Mark and had to part company. Paul persisted in returning to Jerusalem with the offering from the Gentiles when even the Lord himself appeared to him and forbade him to do it. All these sinned. Yet they were not lost. In fact, there is not a single story in the whole Bible of one who was truly a child of God who was lost. Many were overtaken by sin, but none perished."[7]

3.   Perseverance does not mean that those who merely profess Christ without being born again are secure. Specific warnings (which are dealt with in other sections of this book) are given to those who heard the gospel and appeared to trust in Christ, and yet were not truly saved. For example, Jesus said, 'If you abide in my word, you are truly my disciples (John 8:31). This seems to say that perseverance on the part of the believer is the final proof of whether he or she is truly born again. . . our Lord said, 'The one who endures to the end will be saved' (Matt. 10:22). . . . "It is possible to be quite close to Christian things and yet not be truly regenerate."[8]

---

[7] Ibid., 533.

[8] Ibid.

Young Christian

This has been a very helpful discussion. The Bible clearly teaches that God preserves his people all the way until the end. I'm glad we've been able to walk through this doctrine. God definitely gets all the glory for our salvation from enabling us to repent and believe to preserving us all the way till the end. As the reformers put it in the *solas*, *soli deo gloria*!

Questions for
Further Reflection

1. Why is the doctrine of perseverance such a practical teaching?

2. If God sovereignly enables a believer to persevere in the faith, why is it important to simultaneously affirm that there is a race to be run? What would you say about a person who appears to have quit on the race? Why does "endurance" seem to be such a key word in Hebrews?

3. Hebrews 12:1 speaks of a great cloud of witnesses. What are they witnesses to?

4. What did John Owen mean when he said, "Be killing sin or sin will be killing you?" Why is Romans 8:13 such an important admonition in our sanctification?

5. What are some other means of grace that help believers along the path to full and final salvation?

6. Why is "perseverance of the saints" as a label for this doctrine superior to "once saved always saved?" How do Arminian Christians often misunderstand it?

Conclusion

Those He saves are His delight,
Christ will hold me fast.
Precious in His holy sight,
He will hold me fast.

He'll not let my soul be lost,
His promises shall last.
Bought by Him at such a cost
He will hold me fast.[1]

Ask virtually any evangelical pastor what the most popular issue he hears from people in his church and assurance of salvation will surely rank toward

---

[1] Keith and Kristyn Getty, "He Will Hold Me Fast"

the top and it well might occupy the number one spot on the list. But from this dialogue, I hope it's clear that Scripture teaches a genuinely born-again person has no fear of ever facing God's wrath in eternity, for they will never fall away.

Ask Christians if perseverance of the saints is a tier-one issue in the scheme of theological triage, and most will likely say it is a third-tier issue. However, I hope this dialogue has shown that, while believing in perseverance is not a matter of salvation, it is imperative to get right because Scripture is so clear. If genuine Christians can lose their salvation, they will. And if they do, it redefines God and the work of Christ at Calvary and in eternity. This is a problem.

Ask followers of Christ if they've encountered people who seem to have been walking with God at one point only to walk away from Him at another. Most have. A well-known evangelical pastor, a longtime conference speaker, author of many useful books, an adherent to sound doctrine, walks away from his wife, the ministry, and expresses doubts about whether Jesus was God. He writes about deconstructing his faith, how Jesus is still his friend, but no longer the object of his worship, no longer his Savior. He begins to march in Pride Month parades. What do we make of that?

Or a man in your church is seemingly converted out of a longtime pattern of alcohol and drug abuse; his life with Christ flies off the launching pad like a Space X rocket. He shares the gospel with everyone he sees. He attends church every time the doors are open. He contracts a serious illness, and some well-meaning but wrongheaded people in church tell him that if he only claims his healing from God, the illness will vanish like a cast out demon. After all, he's one of the King's kids and the King's family should have impeccable health. After praying for months, his illness grows worse. Healing eludes him. He concludes that Christianity just doesn't work and goes back to the booze and the dope, never to be seen in church again. What happened?

Or a 10-year-old boy seemingly becomes a believer during a spring revival meeting in a Baptist church. He walks with the Lord until age 18 but leaves for college and doesn't take his faith with him. He attends wild parties. He chases girls like there's no tomorrow. He quits church and couldn't locate his Bible with a private detective. Four years later, he has a dramatic turnaround, repenting of his hedonism and returning to regular church attendance and daily Bible reading. He later marries, raises a family, and surrenders to full-time vocational ministry. What happened to him during that period of wilderness wandering? Did he lose his salvation and gain it back again— like a frisbee tossed aside that comes winging back to its pitcher? Was he even converted in the first place until that time after college when he returned, like the prodigal, to Christ?

Granted, these aren't easy questions and the details of every circumstances differ, but as I hope this dialogue has demonstrated, Scripture antici-pates the reality of false conversions and apostates. Unlike us, God is not taken aback by that reality, and He has written about it in His Word. God's Word also makes clear that a genuine Christian will persevere all the way to glory, kept by God's grace. Look at King David. Look at the apos-tle Peter. Apostates and deconstructors do not surprise God and they are present in the Bible. Therefore, if you are truly a follower of Christ, you are safe—even if you come to His kingdom through many dangers, toils, and snares.

Christ the sure and steady Anchor
In the fury of the storm!
When the winds of doubt blow through me,

And my sails have all been torn,
In the suffering, in the sorrow,
When my sinking hopes are few,
I will hold fast to the Anchor
It shall never be removed.[2]

---

[2] Matt Boswell and Matt Papa, "Christ the Sure and Steady Anchor"

About the Author

Jeff Robinson (ABJ, University of Georgia; MDiv, PhD, The Southern Baptist Theological Seminary) serves as president and editor-in-chief of The Baptist Courier and Courier Publishing in Greenville, S.C. A native of Blairsville, Georgia, Jeff is the author or editor of 10 books on ministry, theology, and church history, including *Taming the Tongue: How the Gospel Transforms our Talk* (TGC) and *To the Ends of the Earth: The Missional Vision of John Calvin* (Crossway). Prior to ministry, Jeff worked for 24 years as a newspaper journalist. He has pastored churches in Alabama and Kentucky and serves as adjunct professor of church history at North Greenville University. Jeff and his wife, Lisa, have been married for 30 years and have four grown children. They live in Greenville and belong to Abner Creek Baptist Church in Greer, S.C.

9 781955 295789